I0463090

ECONOMIC
REALITY
&
THE SECRET TO
YOUR
INVESTMENTS

[The Fundamentals of Economics & Money]

DANIEL KRUG

Economic Reality: And The Secret To Your Investments
First Edition

ISBN: 1452814163
ISBN-13: 9781452814162

For additional copies of this book or more information:

contact@danielkrug.com

Please Visit:

www.danielkrug.com

Printed in the United States of America

"New opinions are always suspected, and usually opposed, without any other reason but because they are not already common."

—John Locke

CONTENTS

Introduction   *vii*

Chapter 1: Natural Law   1

Chapter 2: Money   21

Chapter 3: Inflation   41

Chapter 4: The Federal Reserve   61

Chapter 5: Stock Market Gain   77

Chapter 6: Gold Gain   91

Chapter 7: A Secret Pattern   97

Chapter 8: The Secret Key to Your Investments	135

Chapter 9: Why It Works	141

Chapter 10: Why People Will Reject It	149

Chapter 11: Your Investment Portfolio	161

Conclusion	*169*

INTRODUCTION

"It is well that the people of the nation do not understand our banking and monetary system, for if they did, I believe there would be a revolution before tomorrow morning."

—*Henry Ford*

I still remember my first investment. It was an exchange-traded fund (ETF) of emerging markets. At that time, I had limited knowledge of financial markets and how our monetary system worked. I didn't know the fundamentals of investing or what money truly is. I was still young. This was the beginning for me.

I saw the value of that fund rise and fall. It eventually rose, and I sold to realize the gain, but I was more interested *in why* it gained value. This is what sparked my interest in the financial markets. I wanted to learn everything I could about the subject so that I may be able to have future gains on my investments in the future. I was deeply interested in the art of making your money work for you.

From that day forward, I found anything about the economy and monetary policy extremely interesting. Not only did it affect me personally, but I saw how much of an impact it had on everyone's daily life. It affects everything from the daily services a person provides to the things a person buys to make his or her life easier. All people are a part of the economy, whether they believe themselves to be or not. There's no way to get around it.

I studied every aspect of the economy and investing in my personal time. I learned more about economics than anything else that I had previously studied in a formal classroom setting. My personal studies soon began to grow beyond just the financial markets. In order to better understand economic forces, I found that I needed a broader knowledge of why things work the way they do in the world. I soon discovered that economics was not solely about money but extended itself into everything. With economics as my driving force of interest, I soon began studying philosophy, politics, sociology, and religion to better understand everything that affected economics and my investments.

Economics and investing soon became a large enough part of my life that I steered my future career aspirations toward the field of finance. I accepted a position at one of the largest conventional investment firms in the United States as a financial advisor. And so my professional career in finance began.

I worked as a financial advisor and got to see how a typical large investment firm operated. I continued my quest for knowledge and truth about finance, innocently thinking that a large investment firm held such wisdom and knowledge. Through my continued personal economic research, I found the philosophy of large investment companies to be seriously flawed.

The truths about the economy and investing seemed like common sense to me, but the popular financial institutions distorted them. My mind wanted to reject my discoveries (just as you'll want to initially reject the ideas in this book). I wanted to learn from the company I worked for, but I found that a majority of the advice and research from the "smart" investment institutions that everyone was following was actually very faulty and dangerous to their clients. The institution was not truly looking out for the best interests of their clients, but only looking out for itself.

The financial meltdown beginning in 2007 convinced me that everything was wrong. I didn't stop learning. I found other sources to find the truth, and I soon found my philosophical home within the school of Austrian economics. On the contrary, it was obvious that the Keynesian economic philosophy was faulty and had failed. Although there is debate within the Austrian school (which is healthy), they understand and study more of the truth.

I also found a deep interest in studying the investors who forecast the coming of the economic downturn. Did these select few people understand something that everyone else was missing, or were they just lucky? How and why did they know something that everyone else seemed to miss? I studied their philosophies and viewpoints to reveal strong fundamentals that were neglected by the "smart" intellectual economists and investors who failed to forecast the economic depression. Many of these failures are *still* considered the "top" economists of our time and appear regularly on national financial networks.

Many people and organizations would label me as a "contrarian" economist. But, unfortunately, sometimes the truth is labeled as such. Galileo was labeled "contrarian" when he stated the earth was not flat. His thoughts were fiercely rejected. I would rather follow truth than popular belief, if popular belief is a lie.

The current financial industry is drowning in false ideas of investing. Advice is masked in a form that seems great on the surface but destructive in reality. The industry plays on the psychology of the human mind and human nature. Many times, people never discover the truth. With investing, people often take on more risk and receive less return than they actually believe. And if they found out the real risk that they absorbed, there would be an investing revolution in this country.

Some impatient investors may make a short-term gamble and win. People flock toward them and try to imitate them, only to lose their money in highly speculative gambling. The more "sophisticated" investors, proud in thinking they are wise and patient, state that investing for the long term in the stock market helps to reduce risk and produce higher returns. This is wrong. Little do they know that an extremely important economic concept, which we'll learn about in the book, called price inflation destroys *nearly all* of their return. The present monetary policy created by the government and Federal Reserve Bank, along with the popular, yet false, investing ideas of today, has created an increasingly difficult situation for the average person to invest in. Many people do not have the time or the desire to uncover the truths of economics and investing because of the extensive research needed to understand the monetary system, banking system, government policy, and the analysis of which investments are truly better than others.

Here is where I come in. This book condenses all the information, reveals the most important truths and is supported by fundamental laws of economics, historical proof, and current monetary policy. The government, Federal Reserve Bank, media, and especially the large "investment" firms understand these truths and do not want you to read this book. It will transfer profits from them to you. There is an investment pattern revealed in this book that could make investing much easier and help you realize a much higher return on your investments. It is my goal to uncover the truth and provide a resource for people to know where to invest their wealth wisely, giving those people higher returns and assuming less risk.

When reading this book, keep an open mind. Your mind will want to reject many of the subjects and facts in this book. It is going to defy conventional wisdom, meaning that it will state things that have been the opposite of what you were taught about investing throughout your life. The old mantra of saving money in a bank, investing for the long term, etc., is extremely flawed. Try with all your might to accept at least some of these truths. But, if you reject everything just because you were told differently throughout your life, you may continue to live a lie. The truth will set you free. Enjoy.

Daniel Krug

CHAPTER ONE

THE CORNERSTONE: NATURAL LAW

"The natural liberty of man is to be free from any superior power on earth, and not to be under the will or legislative authority of man, but only to have the law of nature for his rule."

—Samuel Adams

You are about to learn an investment strategy that you most likely have never heard of before. After reading this book, I hope that this investment strategy will be helpful, but more importantly, that it will help you realize truths that are not well known in the investment world that may have a great impact on your investment decisions. But before we study economics and investing, we need to delve into something that seems unrelated to economics and investing.

Philosophy seems like it would have no place in the study of economics or a book on investing. However, for economics to be studied in its entirety, philosophy is needed to create a foundation for the basics of economic understanding to be built upon. The foundation should be the first thing studied in order to understand more advanced and smaller aspects of economics and, ultimately, the subject of investing. That is why philosophy is the first topic of discussion in this book.

The fundamental philosophy expressed in this book is called "Natural Law." It is the viewpoint that there is a higher authority in nature that is greater than the laws written and enforced by mankind. Sometimes, mankind makes laws that agree with natural laws, and other times we do not. Whether we try to abide by these natural laws or defy them, we are always held accountable for our decisions. During our lives, we learn that we cannot create a "fantasy land" that appeals to all our desires. There are boundaries and limits which we are always subjected to. It is like the simple math of 1+1=2 and the error of 1+1=3. When we take the microcosm of economics within natural law, we learn that we cannot get something for free. There is no "free lunch". The bill always comes due. There is always a cost, whether it is a transfer of wealth, human labor, etc. Many economists fail to see beyond the initial consequences of economic policies and actions. They often look at the short-term effects, whether it is a month, year, or decade. This error of perception has increased exponentially in our recent history with the popularity of day trading, get rich quick schemes, and unregulated financial activities. Even though economic policies *almost always* have good intentions, it is essential that policy makers and economists look beyond the short-term effects and focus as well on the long-term effects and the unintended consequences throughout the rest of the economy. With natural law as our guide, we view the economy with reason from an abstract viewpoint that accounts for these longer-term effects and consequences that are not as easily predicted.

We do not have authoritative rule as humans, but rather natural law holds authority over us. That is a statement that many people do not like to hear. It is when "catastrophic" events occur that mankind becomes humble once again. In this book, we do not discuss whether that higher authority of natural law is created by God, a chance occurrence, or something we do not understand altogether. That is a separate discussion. But what everyone can agree on, disregarding religious preference or lack thereof, is that natural law is *real*, and we are bound by it whether we understand it, live by it, or neglect it. It is the neglect of this very fact that hides the truth about all things, including economics.

Within the study and acknowledgement of natural law itself, we find smaller conflicting ideas within. Philosophers such as Descartes, Hobbes, Locke, and many others have studied and written about natural law throughout history. Regardless of the difference in the study of natural law, they all agree that there in fact is a general natural law. Natural law in general helps identify the foundation to the understanding of the subjects in this book. It also shows why the statements of some "intelligent" investors have failed throughout history (tulip boom & bust, India Sea Co.) and today (housing bubble, dollar crash). There are so many misconceptions and reasons that have led people to forget the simple and fundamental laws that govern all things on earth, including their investments. This book tells of a fundamental philosophy that supports economic understanding and the secret key to investing that we will learn about later in this book.

BASICS OF NATURAL LAW

We all remember the rules our parents demanded we follow. We knew that if we did not follow the rules, there would be consequences. Sometimes, when a parent, teacher, or other human-related entity (like government) does not elect to honestly enforce their rules, a person can get around or avoid the consequences. However, there are rules in life that cannot be broken and must be followed no matter the desire to defy them. They are enforced not by man, who sometimes has weaknesses in enforcing rules or when the rules themselves change, but are enforced by something much greater than man. There are always consequences to breaking the rules of this authority. This is natural law.

Natural law is the foundation of everything in this world. We live in nature and must abide by its rules. We cannot escape our earthly environment until the day we die and therefore are under its rule for the duration of our lives. Natural law includes all the rules that are not of human creation. They have been here since the creation and will be here until the end of time. This goes beyond laws found in wildlife as the word "natural" may indicate. It applies to everything, such as human nature, mathematics, and it even applies to economics. If it were not, man could change laws of economics to whatever he decided is best for him. Because of the evil ambitions of greed, corruption, and aggression, which are sometimes found in the minds of tyrants, we are constantly reminded of our economic folly when we defy natural law. Historical proof and common sense show that man does not make the natural laws that everyone must follow, but we must form our societies and economies to the will of natural law. If economics could be created by man, there would be a utopia in which no poverty existed and no human labor was needed. Keynesian economics gravitates toward this theory.

Keynesian economics is a theory that is surprisingly accepted as truth by our government officials and "leading economists" in universities today that make our current economic decisions. The man who created the philosophy, John Maynard Keynes, was proven wrong in the 1970s as Milton Friedman made a fool of him using basic common sense. However, we still follow his ideas on a policy level. It is a theory based upon the blatant negligence of natural law. Obviously, an economic and social utopia will never be possible on Earth in the way the Keynesian economists wish. We know that to create wealth, there needs to be production and human labor in certain areas of the economic society. However, Keynesians state that spending on unemployment creates jobs and is a step forward. We should know that there are some people who are willing to work hard and some who prefer to be lazy. There are those who take risks and those who are more conservative. There are those with great ideas and others with not such great ideas. There are those who are honest and those who are dishonest. We know and have seen in history that each is rewarded as such, thus creating a difference in wealth of property and influence. We are created equal in the sense that we all have the inalienable rights declared in our Declaration of Independence. But, we are most definitely not equal in our abilities and actions. We, as humans, did not make these rules up ourselves. These rules were established through our human nature as a society. If we neglect them we suffer the consequences.

Fundamentally, natural law governs everything. It is immovable and constant. It has been this way since the beginning of time. When government is established by man to protect life, liberty, and property as our Declaration of Independence declares and the laws are harmonious with natural laws, the country will flourish by increasing every person's standard of living and freedom. When mankind tries to live by its own rules that *defy* natural law, that group of men experience the negative consequences.

We should place natural law as a cornerstone to our understanding of economics and investing. Throughout this book, natural laws of economics are revealed. Complex investments have no true basis if the fundamentals are flawed. Therefore, learning the fundamentals, first, is essential, even if it gives us the feeling of learning something elementary. Modern consensus states that learning complex investing systems within economics makes a person smart and profitable. It is not necessarily so and often has the obverse effect. The simple and fundamental is essential to knowledge and wisdom. A surgeon must learn about cell structure before conducting heart surgery. Pilots must study aerodynamics and physics before they are to fly airplanes. Without the basics you are destined for failure. With the basics, you can always expand upon that solid foundation. If we can conclude that basics are essential, then I wonder how much the "investment gurus" really knew about investing at all, if they suggested rising housing prices were perpetual and mortgage-backed securities were safe investments in the recent economic bust. They obviously focused too much of their attention on complex ideas and left no study for the fundamentals. Fundamental natural law shows us the road to prosperity for ourselves, for our country, and for the world.

To *truly* understand something requires a complete breakdown of its simplest components. For example, when a scientist attempts to understand the human body, the understanding of the simpler and smaller components (cells, atoms, etc.) is essential to understand the complex and larger issue at hand (ex: disease). When we break down to the fundamental components, we as humans come to one of two conclusions. Either we do *not* understand the fundamentals due to our limited knowledge, or we find that the fundamentals are ultimately governed by natural law (ex: gravity, electricity, etc). It is important to know that the things we do *not* understand are still governed by natural law. However, we have not yet been able to understand it (ex: cure for cancer, black holes, dark matter, etc). It may take a bit of humility to accept the fact that we are not all knowing creatures of our environment. Throughout history, we have been able to expand our knowledge and understand more of these natural laws. And some of the things that we thought to be true for centuries turned out to be false! Regardless, we have been able to use our knowledge and industry to produce a higher standard of living. Whether we understand something in our environment or not, we can conclude that *everything is governed by nature, even if we do not understand it*.

When we learn, understand, and live by natural laws, we will have prosperity. Nature holds both endless possibilities and boundaries for mankind at the same time. In order to understand anything, you must first understand nature. What I mean by understanding natural law is being able to understand basic rules that govern everything from basic human interaction to subjects such as economics while being able to disregard conventional "wisdom" that defies it. Anything that you wish to fully understand must be broken up into these basic components, which are governed by natural law. Even trying to understand a subject dealing with human interaction is the attempt at understanding the natural laws of humanity. By studying natural law, you know you are studying the truth and the unmanipulative creation of God (or the universe, for non-believers). There are endless possibilities for construction and discovery by man that we have not even begun to imagine. However, at the same time, boundaries still exist. In regards to economics, these basic truths are sometimes neglected or perceived as unbelievable to the general public, but we must acknowledge them as truth.

NATURAL LAW OF ECONOMICS

It is a common misconception that an economy is *created* by people. It is not. Economy, when studying its most basic components, is found to contain only natural law. The natural laws of economics are very basic and are attributed to the individual choices of mankind that are unknown to the whole of mankind itself. In most circumstances it is the law of equality and the law of virtue.

The natural law of equality applies to various areas of the economy. A successful business must have more income than expenses to survive. If that is not the case, it can no longer be in business. *(Why would a government think bailing out a company that is bankrupt as a good thing?)* It is a simple equation and common sense, yet many people overlook the simplicity and focus on minute details. The same applies to government. *Does our government follow that same rule of law?* If the government does not abide by this law, it will accrue a debt and eventually have to either pay it off through being very frugal and increasing taxes or, if it controls the currency, destroy the currency to monetize the debt (printing of money to pay off debt). In the realm of investing, if there is a high return on an investment, the law of equality states that there must be a relatively equal amount of risk. The law of equality is simple, yet very often ignored, due to mankind's lack of respect for simplicity, fundamentals, and an abstract view of nature.

The natural law of virtue in economics states that doing good service for others will bring wealth back to you. The most successful people often provide a service or product, because they enjoy it and want to be able to *help* others live a better life. Their enthusiasm for their product and enthusiasm for helping others helps them to overcome obstacles and adversities that are inevitable in business and life. Sometimes this happens without the business owner ever knowing it because it is subconscious. If it were just about the money, their business would most likely fail. A better economy represents not only positive political will but virtue in its participants. Without the desire to help others and build a business, economies cannot expand. That is why it says in many religions that in order to acquire riches, you must first give.

The famous economic idea of supply and demand is so basic that it is the foundation for almost all economic theory. It is another name for the law of equality. There is constant fluctuation of balancing between supply and demand; risk and reward. This fluctuation is another reason why a utopian-style economy goes against natural law. Supply and demand is a great example of not only the law of equality but of the law of virtue as well. If there is no demand for the product that someone created, it will fail *to serve* society and cease to exist. There will be no supply, simply because it is not beneficial to anyone. There needs to be a relatively equal amount of desire for an equal amount of production. Everything created needs to be created for the desire of society. If it is not, no one will buy it, and no one will make a living selling it. In socialistic-style economies, where the governmental body makes decisions, there is often production in areas with no demand and limited production in areas that are needed. This decreases the living standard of its own citizens. The ordered chaos of individual wants and needs creates a prosperous and better economy.

The act of business is inherently good. The reward is profit. It is a profit that is eventually used to promote even more business and good in society. Unfortunately, in our country today, there is a misconception of how someone gained profit. Profit is often misunderstood as someone having found success at the expense of others or through some avenue of evil activity. The media in our society today tells us that money is evil. This viewpoint is politically driven to win votes. Although there are a few unfortunate instances of evil in profits which is highly publicized, the reality is that the vast majority of profitable people provide a service or product that makes many other people's lives *better*. If a person does *not serve* society in a way that is virtuous, that person will be forced to change employment to an area that does. Money is not the root of all evil. The *love* of money is.

In regards to investing, during the 1990s and early 2000s, housing prices were going through the roof (no pun intended). Some people said that housing prices could *"never"* go down. In retrospect, it's easier to see why that was such an ignorant statement. But at the time, almost all of the "intellectual elite investors" believed and announced that real estate was a win-win investment, because it always increased in value! This went *against* the laws of nature. However, people were easily fooled. The historical housing price trends didn't add up. If housing prices continued to rise at a rapid pace, higher than inflation (greater than the demand), and ignored the ability to pay loans by the borrowers, natural law forced a point of exhaustion in that sector. It was obvious that it could not possibly continue. The consequence was an inevitable and obvious crash. Here are some comments from the "experts" during that time period:

Chapter One: The Cornerstone: Natural Law

"Those who argue that housing prices are now at a point of a bubble seem to me to be missing a very important point. Unlike previous examples we have had when substantial excessive inflation of prices later caused problems we are talking here about an entity, home ownership, homes where there is not the degree of leverage where we have seen elsewhere. This is not the dot-com situation. We had problems with people having invested in business plans of which there was no reality; people building fiber optic cables for which there was no need. Homes that are occupied may see an ebb and flow in the price at a certain percentage level. But you're not going to see the collapse that you see when people talk about a bubble and so those of us on our committee in particular will continue to push for home ownership."

—Barney Frank, House Financial Services Committee, June 27, 2005 (Re-elected)

"House prices have risen by nearly 25 percent over the past two years. Although speculative activity has increased in some areas, at a national level these price increases largely reflect strong economic fundamentals, including robust growth in jobs and incomes, low mortgage rates, steady rates of household formation, and factors that limit the expansion of housing supply in some areas."
—Ben Bernanke, Federal Reserve Chairman, October 5, 2005 (Presently still serves in his capacity as Chairman)

"Although we certainly cannot rule out home price declines, especially in some local markets, these declines, were they to occur, likely would not have substantial macroeconomic implications.

13

Nationwide banking and widespread securitization of mortgages make it less likely that financial intermediation would be impaired than was the case in prior episodes of regional house price corrections."

—Alan Greenspan, Former Federal Reserve Chairman, June 8, 2005

These "intelligent" men neglected natural law and basic fundamentals. And yet they are the leaders and top economists that make very important decisions about our economic policy and way of life. *Are you kidding me? This is the best we got?*

Going back to the natural law of economics, is it not common sense that if you spend more than you take in, negative consequences will occur (law of equality)? Will it not end in poverty? If someone creates something that does not benefit society, is it sustainable (law of virtue)? People perceive complex investments to be profitable on the sole fact that it is difficult to understand them. Mortgage-backed securities, which many people knew nothing about, were thought to be very profitable investments. It crashed. Never did investors think that an ever-rising real estate sector would hit a point of exhaustion. They did not see that nature was the ruling force of everything including the economy. Basic fundamentals of the economy are easily understood and should not be cast aside as ideas of antiquity or too simple for application. The laws of nature never go out of style. They govern us all and for all time.

Understanding the natural laws of economics and investing is *much* more valuable than understanding what a mortgage-backed security is. If you knew that, you most likely would not have been exposed to the real-estate bubble. If you can find a way for your mind to agree that simple natural laws rule everything, including the economy, then you are on the first step to understanding truth and realizing a greater return on your investments. It is dangerous to follow investment advice and investment books that do not address the basic fundamentals and only apply manipulated data from a small period of time that supports their theory. The next time you read or hear financial advice, think about the more fundamental aspect of what they are referencing and if it is in compliance with natural law. It is a must that you apply this philosophy to economics and investing as a cornerstone to your understanding.

NATURAL LAW IN POLITICS (REGARDING ECONOMICS)

"The natural progress of things is for liberty to yield and government to gain ground."

—*Thomas Jefferson*

It is inevitable that politics will affect economic policy. Whether that policy aids or hurts the economy is a different aspect. But through history and nature, we can see what works and what does not.

When government has limited influence upon the economy, prosperity is found. The fluctuations in supply and demand are not always known and foreseen by mankind and bureaucrats in government. The individual choices of so many people cannot be controlled from a central, authoritative entity, because it will distort the real supply and demands, which would create a better standard of living based upon an individual person's needs and desires. Economic freedom looks like chaos, but it is actually orderly.

Therefore, the government should do it's best to not regulate free markets, or the economy will experience negative consequences. Demand will exceed supply, and supply will exceed demand in different sectors. Laws of equality and virtue should be free to reign as well as the individual choices of people that essentially drive an economy.

A great historical example of the positives of free markets with limited government intervention is with the beginning of the United States. The economy was relatively free, and the standard of living continued to increase rapidly. Because of the proposition by the founding fathers, especially Thomas Jefferson's Declaration of Independence (which was considered at that time to be extremely radical) that individual choices and property rights were essential to their lives, the free market exploded to provide prosperity never before seen in the history of mankind. We still are reaping the rewards of this system.

The current U.S. political climate has changed in regards to economics and the natural law upon which it was founded. Presently, there is more central power and influence over the economy. There are countless regulations and restrictions that stifle economic growth and freedom. The tax code itself is over 54,000 pages long. In perspective, there was NO income tax before 1913 (except during the civil war). That is a huge difference! The government's attempt at manipulating the natural laws of economics will surely result in negative consequences, some of which we have experienced and many of which we have yet to experience.

Historically, large government repetitively tries to manipulate natural law to benefit themselves politically and monetarily at the expense of the citizens. That is why the United States of America, when first created, produced prosperity that the world had never seen. It was a very small government with emphasis on local and individual rights. This was unprecedented and allowed for natural law to flourish. Many people often cannot fathom the tyranny and economic hardship before the founding of our country, because we never had first-hand experience with it. Never before in history had a country been founded on true freedom of religion, speech, commerce, and civil rights. It was a nation founded on small, limited government, which was ruled not by elites or aristocracies, but by the individual and natural law (although this has changed). The founding fathers believed in God and studied natural laws intensely.

*"Man. . .hath by nature a power. . .to pressure his property— that is, **his life, liberty, and estate**—against the injuries and attempts of other men."*

—*John Locke, 1690, Essay Concerning Human Understanding, Book 2, Chapter 21, p171*

*"We hold these truths to be self-evident, that all men are created equal, that they are endowed by their **Creator** with certain unalienable Rights, that among these are **Life, Liberty, and the Pursuit of Happiness."***

—*Thomas Jefferson, Declaration of Independence, 1776*

From their belief sprouted a great country of prosperity and freedom that we still feel the effects of today. It overflowed into other nations through our leadership by example. When other countries saw the wealth it created, they followed suit. That is why the Chinese adopted a semi-capitalist economy in the 1980s which propelled them to become an economic superpower today. Therefore, republics replaced dictators, kings and queens, and other tyrants. It made the world a better place. Think what the world would be like today without the existence of America and her beacon of freedom.

It would surely be a world of hardship and lower living standards. However, now, America is traveling down a dangerous path. Most of us have forgotten history and ignored God and natural law. We expect the economy to continue to prosper regardless of policy.

Many times, the efforts of the manipulation of natural laws by large governments are masked in the name of good intentions. This is how it is accepted by the public. There is a famous saying of *"The road to hell is paved with good intentions."* It is the ignorance and lack of understanding that results in the negative consequences. In the end, *natural law will overcome*. It is very simple, yet people often forget the simple rules of nature. People often mistake complex investment instruments, "good" deficits, and government bureaucrats to be more advanced and know better than the laws of nature. A Yale or Harvard doctorate degree does not grant the ability to defy natural laws, no matter how smart a central person or entity believes he or she is.

In the next chapter we will have a narrower focus on economics. This chapter may have been difficult to read. The subject of natural law is overflowing with philosophical viewpoints and opinions that include and exclude economics. The point that I hope reached you is that unnatural things cannot be reality no matter how hard we try to make them as such. This includes economics and investing. This is the foundation of the ideas in this book. Now, we will journey further into economics.

SUMMARY

Truth #1: Natural Law Governs Everything...Including Economics

- Natural Law governs everything
- Natural Law applies to economics
    - Man cannot manipulate laws of economics
    - This includes economic laws such as the law of equality and the law of virtue

CHAPTER TWO

MONEY

"I, however, place economy among the first and most important republican virtues, and public debt as the greatest of the dangers to be feared."

—*Thomas Jefferson*

WHAT IS MONEY?

When thinking of investing, people often have serious questions about stocks, bonds, mutual funds, banks, and other assets that deal with what they perceive to be worth a certain monetary value. But rarely do people ask the more fundamental question of, *"What is money?"* In order to understand what a stock, bond, or asset is, let alone how to analyze those investments, a person must first focus his or her attention on the fundamentals.

". . .the loftiest edifices need the deepest foundations."

—George Santayana

When someone asks you how much money you have, how do you answer? You would most likely answer in the amount of dollars you have. Many U.S. citizens believe money to simply be the dollars in their wallet or their money in the bank. This is a general assumption that holds an important but widely believed *falsehood*. Money is not a dollar, but something much more naturally fundamental.

Money is purchasing power.

Something has purchasing power when a person is able to exchange the form or substitute of the money for a good or service that they need or want. In our society, most believe that the dollar is money, but in reality fundamentals say it is purchasing power.

In our era, most people think it would be silly to work for $2 an hour. Two dollars won't purchase much! However, many people are falsely led to believe that it is the number *(nominal amount)* of dollars that matters in a person's assessment of his or her wealth. It is not! It is the purchasing power that is important. *(Now you are probably thinking this guy is crazy! You most likely would* say, *"of course $100,000 is more than $50,000!"* You would be correct, but only in nominal terms. If I introduce time into the equation, the nominal figures stay the same, but the *real* value will change! The same U.S. dollar in 1913 would have purchased about 1/750 of a house. Today it will purchase about 1/150,000 of a house. In both instances, they have the same nominal value, but the purchasing power *(real value)* is different.

Here's another example. Zimbabwe has recently been through economic turmoil and has experienced massive hyperinflation. In Zimbabwe, eventually a 100 trillion-dollar bill from their central bank is worth almost nothing! With logical thought, this must reveal that the nominal value does not matter. Rather, it is the purchasing power *(real value)* that truly matters. It is extremely important to think of money as something that has purchasing power, not just a nominal amount. Unfortunately, thinking of money as a nominal amount has been ingrained into our societal thinking because it is advantageous to a certain group. But you must break free of this misconception of fundamentals in order to understand the rest of the book. It doesn't matter if money is a dollar, silver, or a diamond. Anything that has purchasing power is money. *Money is purchasing power.* I cannot stress this enough.

Once we receive money (purchasing power) in exchange for our labor, we either save it, purchase goods, or want the money to be used in a way in which it will grow and help society at the same time. The latter is called investing. Some investors may buy real estate or start businesses, which are great ways to invest if done wisely. Another popular way of investing is when people invest their money through already established companies (like through our stock market). Whatever the case is, *all investors assume risk*. Believe it or not, even people who just want to hold their purchasing power in currency denominated savings (like putting money in the bank) assume risk, because the purchasing power of the money can change over time. Later, you will see how *terrible* of a place the bank is to store your wealth. It is my mission to educate the average person on how he or she can invest and assume *less risk* with *higher returns*, which previously may have invested in the stock market or put his or her money in the bank. It is taking advantage of this common misconception made by millions of investors. But first, we need to study the fundamentals of what we are trying to understand. We need to understand the basic history of how money evolved.

HISTORY OF MONEY

"The desire of gold is not for gold. It is for the means of freedom and benefit."
—Ralph Waldo Emerson

As we learned, money is a vehicle that represents purchasing power. It can be the dollar, gold, oil, or a watch! Anything that holds purchasing power and can be exchanged for something is money! It is also important to know the history of money. What makes money have purchasing power and what qualities does it hold? How has it transformed? We can discover these truths by researching history and how money has evolved through the immovable forces of natural law.

In the beginning of human history, the first economic transactions were done in what was called *bartering*. This is where tangible products were exchanged for other tangible products. An example of bartering would be a shepherd exchanging one of his sheep for an axe made by the blacksmith. Both parties are satisfied. However, as an economy expands, this becomes increasingly more inefficient. An example of the inefficiency is if the axe that the blacksmith makes is only worth the value of half a sheep *and* the blacksmith lives on the other side of town! This proves to be difficult because the shepherd is forced to slaughter his sheep in half and carry half the sheep across town to the blacksmith. The second half of the sheep not used to purchase the axe needs to be instantly eaten or traded for something else because it will rot. What if the blacksmith does not need half a sheep but needs fish instead? The shepherd would have to trade his sheep for fish *and then* trade for the axe. Do you see how this becomes a problem? *That's not an efficient money system!* Over time, due to the increase of complex trade and economies, a form of universal purchasing power has evolved…*a money system*. Its evolution has been governed by natural law.

Natural law has chosen gold and silver as the best form of money. Gold and silver eventually became money because of its amicability with the natural law of money and economy. Good, sound money for a developed economy has qualities that make the system of exchanging purchasing power *more efficient and true!* In place of the actual tangible goods (ex: sheep), a different medium of exchange is used that is valued by *all* participants in the economy. They can exchange their goods for the gold or silver and then go and purchase *any other* amount of product with the same precious metals. It constructs the most efficient money market system. Look at each quality of sound money below and take the time to think of *why* they are needed in a complex economic system. Here are the qualities a universal, sound-money substitute requires:

1) Luxury Item/Scarcity—*little is needed to exchange and is universally desired*
2) Portability—*able to be carried*
3) Durable—*cannot rot or be destroyed easily*
4) Homogenous—*same quality throughout*
5) Divisibility—*easily separated into smaller and larger value*
6) Limited Supply/Not Seasonal—*supply cannot be increased in massive quantities and is not seasonal, therefore staying relatively the same value*

7) Cognoscibility—*able to stamp for official minting purposes*

If you think back to the example of the shepherd and his sheep, the sheep meets almost none of these qualities. That is why it is not a good substitute for money. You don't see people carrying around sheep to pay for things! It needs to be more efficient. This is why money has evolved. As you can see, gold and silver hold all of these qualities remarkably well. It is the reason why precious metals have been used as money for *thousands* of years. Yes…*thousands.* Think of any other object that can be used as money and see if it meets the requirements. It is natural law that demands these requirements. You will be surprised to find nothing compares to the ability of precious metals such as silver and gold to be the best form of money. Even the "almighty" U.S. dollar (which is paper) does not hold well to #1, #3, #5, and #6. *(So if the dollar does not follow the rules of natural law for sound money (like the sheep), why is it used as money? Why do we use it?))* Be patient. We'll answer that question later.

It is against "popular" thought to think of gold as money. If you were constantly exposed to this "popular" thought, then right now, you are probably trying to come up with every argument *against* gold as being money. *(Oh, you're just a nut. Money can never be gold! You can't eat gold! The dollar has always been money. You're just a doomsday person.)* This is a normal human emotion when confronting something that opposes what you have been taught and practiced throughout your life. I urge you to think clearly, logically, and honestly about the truths in this book. If you neglect this truth, you most likely will oppose many of the following truths in this book. Unfortunately, it will be to your detriment in the form of your wealth and prosperity.

It is only factual to acknowledge that paper currencies have failed throughout history. However, gold does not depend upon which country or government is in power like paper currency demands. It does not end by inflationary measures (Weimar Republic, Zimbabwe) or by monetary transition (Euro). It is a universal currency and has been in place since complex economies demanded more efficiency in the form of money thousands of years ago. HISTORY, MONETARY EVOLUTION, AND THE NATURAL LAW OF SOUND MONEY REVEAL THAT GOLD AND OTHER PRECIOUS METALS ARE REAL MONEY!

MONEY SUBSTITUTE LIFE SPANS

American Dollar: 150+ years

Gold: 2,800+ years

From a historical standpoint,
which do you have more faith in?

MONETARY DEBASEMENT

*"Gold is to monetary policy what the
North Star is to determining location."*

—*Steve Forbes*

As you know, if you take out your wallet, you realize that we do not currently use precious metals such as gold for money. *(If gold and silver are such good forms of money, why do we use dollars instead?)* The reason why our currency is no longer gold or silver is because governments (including ours) try to control and manipulate money in order to benefit itself and its special interests at the expense of the citizens (we'll learn more about that later). There are countless books that are solely devoted to this subject, so I will leave further information on that subject for those who would like to research more themselves. I am only going to state the basic information needed to understand the larger picture. We are going to learn about the history of some governmental monetary policies and their tendencies, which represent the general effect of governmental monetary control.

Governments throughout history have repeatedly altered the sound money of precious metals to benefit themselves. They demand use of their own paper currency, which is manipulated and destroys the wealth of the citizens. However, throughout failed currencies, money has always returned to its nature; that is, gold and silver. Here is a classic historical example of what monetary debasement is:

MONETARY DEBASEMENT IN THE ROMAN EMPIRE

The Roman Empire lasted over one millennium. That's a long time! It is much longer than the existence of the United States to date. To compare, the United States has only been in existence for less than three centuries (three-tenths of the Roman Empire). However, like many large governments, the Roman Empire eventually tried to manipulate the currency. Negative consequences were the result.

As early as the rule of Nero (54-68 A.D.) there is evidence that the demand for revenue led to debasement of the coinage. Revenue was needed to pay the increasing costs of defense and a growing bureaucracy. However, rather than raise taxes, Nero and subsequent emperors preferred to debase the currency by reducing the precious metal content of coins. This was, of course, a form of taxation; in this case, a tax on cash balances (Bailey 1956).

Throughout most of the Empire, the basic units of Roman coinage were the gold aureus, the silver denarius, and the copper or bronze sesterce. [8] The aureus was minted at 40-42 to the pound, the denarius at 84 to the pound, and a sesterce was equivalent to one-quarter of a denarius. Twenty-five denarii equaled one aureus and the denarius was considered the basic coin and unit of account.

The aureus did not circulate widely. Consequently, debasement was mainly limited to the denarius. Nero reduced the silver content of the denarius to 90 percent and slightly reduced the size of the aureus in order to maintain the 25 to 1 ratio. Trajan (98-117 A.D.) reduced the silver content to 85 percent, but was able to maintain the ratio because of a large influx of gold. In fact, some historians suggest that he deliberately devalued the denarius, precisely in order to maintain the historic ratio. Debasement continued under the reign of Marcus Aurelius (161-180 A.D.), who reduced the silver content of the denarius to 75 percent, further reduced by Septimius Severus to 50 percent. By the middle of the third century A.D., the denarius had a silver content of just 5 percent.

Interestingly, the continual debasements did not improve the Empire's fiscal position. This is because of Gresham's Law ("bad money drives out good"). People would hoard older, high-silver content coins and pay their taxes in those with the least silver. Thus the government's "real" revenues may have actually fallen. As Aurelio Bernardi explains:

At the beginning, the debasement proved undoubtedly profitable for the state. Nevertheless, in the course of years, this expedient was abused and the [fn2] century of inflation which had been thus brought about was greatly to the disadvantage of the State's finances. Prices were rising too rapidly and it became impossible to count on an immediate proportional increase in the fiscal revenue, because of the rigidity of the apparatus of tax collection.

Bruce Bartlett, *"How Excessive Government Killed Ancient Rome",* CATO Journal, Volume 14 Number 2, Fall 1994

The people were forced to use the government's coinage and, therefore, the government kept more of the *true* wealth (silver) but still had the "legal" coins worth that same nominal value. The same nominal value amount deceived the people into thinking that they had the same amount of money. The winner was the government and the loser was the person holding the currency. For the government, it seemed pretty smart to get something for nothing! However, it proved to be one of the contributing factors to the downfall of the Roman Empire (Remember the Roman Empire lasted for a thousand years). Three centuries later, the

Roman currency (denarius) had only 5 percent silver content when it was finally no longer used because it was inherently worthless. The citizens lost their wealth. Although they had the same *nominal amount* of the currency, it was worth much less in its *real value*. The debt incurred by the government proved to be too great for the empire to survive. The Roman Empire eventually fell, which had previously ruled for many centuries.

In order for there to be prosperity in a country, there must be honesty in the form of money that is used. Many countries throughout history have repeated this same mistake of debasing the currency. The results are similar. *History repeats itself* because man has qualities and faults that they do not correct across generational time gaps. It is attributed to the ignorance of governments and the people who do not demand the necessary and constant change back to a sound money form—the acknowledgement of natural law.

You may have realized when reading this chapter, that the United States seems to be following a very similar economic path to that of the Roman Empire. We have enormous amounts of debts and obligations and have continued to devalue and debase the currency. (*Are we going to be like the Roman Empire economically?*) If we stay on this path, it is inevitable in time, unless drastic changes are made. Most Americans have lived their lives thinking that nothing bad can happen economically, because it will only get better as it has in the recent past. Well, that is only because the current living generations have experienced a very good economy relative to history. They have never experienced otherwise. So, in our minds, it is illogical to contemplate the opposite. But, if you just look at the facts and the numbers, the writing is on the wall. The only unknown question that cannot be answered is *when* it will happen, unless a major change occurs toward natural law, which is currently political suicide.

To think the economy of the United States is immune to economic collapse is to ignore history, natural law, and common sense (this is yet again a topic that will test your resolve to challenge "popular wisdom"). Every economy in history has failed in the sense of keeping wealth constant in *real* terms. France is still France, but they have defaulted on their debt numerous times throughout history and have changed their currency as well. The denarius of Rome has changed to individual currencies of the European countries and has changed once again so it is now a united currency called the Euro. As investors, we must study history, natural law, and human nature to look ahead and defend ourselves, our wealth, and investments.

A PERSONAL EXPERIENCE: MONETARY DEBASEMENT OF THE UNITED STATES

"Paper money has had the effect in your state that it will ever have, to ruin commerce, oppress the honest, and open the door to every species of fraud and injustice."

—*George Washington*

That quote is from one of the most respected figures in American history. Yet, the very thing that he detests has his face printed on it and is distributed throughout the country that he helped form!

The United States currency had at one time consisted of gold and silver. It was traded mostly in the form of physical coin. During the revolution, paper currency was tried (the continental), was inflated, and failed. (This is where the phrase "not worth a continental" came from.) Real wealth and our currency returned to precious metals. However, a century later, to help finance the civil war, the United States again reverted back to paper currency. Afterwards, the currency returned to sound money in the form of gold-backed paper. This time, the paper currency was redeemable in silver and gold which basically brought about a gold standard once again. The paper currency was only used to represent real gold that was held in another place. At any time, a person with a dollar could theoretically exchange it for *real* gold and silver. The government was restrained on spending because there was and still is a relatively finite amount of gold (since gold cannot be mass produced like paper). It created prosperity never before seen on Earth because of fiscal morality from government and the people. This type of money system lasted up to the early 20th century. Many collectors still have these dollars that state the redemption of gold or silver on the bottom of the dollar bill (even though the government has reneged on that obligation of exchange).

This money system of gold and silver drastically changed in the year 1933. In the midst of the great depression, President Roosevelt proclaimed an "executive order" that all people with possession of gold had to surrender it to a Federal Reserve member bank (the central bank). The president needed a way to fund the enormous expansion of government public programs, entitlements, and other regulations to "help" the economy recover from the great depression. All gold was taken by force from the people! It was stolen by our own president! With that executive order by the president, there was a fine of owning gold at $10,000 ($160,000 in today's dollars) and/or ten years in prison! Today's dollars are neither backed by gold nor silver. It is *only paper!*

Later, the coinage act of 1965 further debased the United States coinage. Up until 1965, coins had actual silver content of 90 percent. Now, there is *no silver content* in our coins. I bet if you look at the change you receive when you purchase things, you will *not* find pre-1965 quarters or dimes. They are worth *much more* (because of their silver content) than the face value (10 cents or 25 cents). The result is that they are taken out of circulation by collectors and only used according to the worth of their silver content. It all reverts back to natural law. The reduction of the silver content or any commodity base in the coins is debasing money (making it worth less).

POSTMASTER: PLEASE POST IN A CONSPICUOUS PLACE.—JAMES A. FARLEY, Postmaster General

UNDER EXECUTIVE ORDER OF THE PRESIDENT

issued April 5, 1933

all persons are required to deliver

ON OR BEFORE MAY 1, 1933

all GOLD COIN, GOLD BULLION, AND GOLD CERTIFICATES now owned by them to a Federal Reserve Bank, branch or agency, or to any member bank of the Federal Reserve System.

Executive Order

FORBIDDING THE HOARDING OF GOLD COIN, GOLD BULLION AND GOLD CERTIFICATES.

By virtue of the authority vested in me by Section 5(b) of the Act of October 6, 1917, as amended by Section 2 of the Act of March 9, 1933, entitled "An Act to provide relief in the existing national emergency in banking, and for other purposes", in which amendatory Act Congress declared that a serious emergency exists, I, Franklin D. Roosevelt, President of the United States of America, do declare that said national emergency still continues to exist and pursuant to said section do hereby prohibit the hoarding of gold coin, gold bullion, and gold certificates within the continental United States by individuals, partnerships, associations and corporations and hereby prescribe the following regulations for carrying out the purposes of this order:

Section 1. For the purposes of this regulation, the term "hoarding" means the withdrawal and withholding of gold coin, gold bullion or gold certificates from the recognized and customary channels of trade. The term "person" means any individual, partnership, association or corporation.

Section 2. All persons are hereby required to deliver on or before May 1, 1933, to a Federal reserve bank or a branch or agency thereof or to any member bank of the Federal Reserve System all gold coin, gold bullion and gold certificates now owned by them or coming into their ownership on or before April 28, 1933, except the following:

(a) Such amount of gold as may be required for legitimate and customary use in industry, profession or art within a reasonable time, including gold prior to refining and stocks of gold in reasonable amounts for the usual trade requirements of owners mining and refining such gold.

(b) Gold coin and gold certificates in an amount not exceeding in the aggregate $100.00 belonging to any one person; and gold coins having a recognized special value to collectors of rare and unusual coins.

(c) Gold coin and bullion earmarked or held in trust for a recognized foreign government or foreign central bank or the Bank for International Settlements.

(d) Gold coin and bullion licensed for other proper transactions (not involving hoarding) including gold coin and bullion imported for reexport or held pending action on applications for export licenses.

Section 3. Until otherwise ordered any person becoming the owner of any gold coin, gold bullion, or gold certificates after April 28, 1933, shall within three days deliver thereof, deliver the same in the manner prescribed in Section 2, unless such gold coin, gold bullion or gold certificates are held for any of the purposes specified in paragraphs (a), (b) or (c) of Section 2, or unless such gold coin or gold bullion is held for purposes specified in paragraph (d) of Section 2 and the person holding it is, with respect to such gold coin or bullion, a licensee or applicant for license pending action thereon.

Section 4. Upon receipt of gold coin, gold bullion or gold certificates delivered to it in accordance with Sections 2 or 3, the Federal reserve bank or member bank will pay therefor an equivalent amount of any other form of coin or currency coined or issued under the laws of the United States.

Section 5. Member banks shall deliver all gold coin, gold bullion and gold certificates owned or received by them (other than as exempted under the provisions of Section 2) to the Federal reserve banks of their respective districts and receive credit or payment therefor.

Section 6. The Secretary of the Treasury, out of the sum made available to the President by Section 501 of the Act of March 9, 1933, will in all proper cases pay the reasonable costs of transportation of gold coin, gold bullion or gold certificates delivered to a member bank or Federal reserve bank in accordance with Sections 2, 3, or 5 hereof, including the cost of insurance, protection, and such other incidental costs as may be necessary, upon production of satisfactory evidence of such costs. Voucher forms for this purpose may be procured from Federal reserve banks.

Section 7. In cases where the delivery of gold coin, gold bullion or gold certificates by the owners thereof within the time set forth above will involve extraordinary hardship or difficulty, the Secretary of the Treasury may, in his discretion, extend the time within which such delivery must be made. Applications for such extensions must be made in writing under oath, addressed to the Secretary of the Treasury and filed with a Federal reserve bank. Each application must state the date to which the extension is desired, the amount and location of the gold coin, gold bullion and gold certificates in respect of which such application is made and the facts showing extension to be necessary to avoid extraordinary hardship or difficulty.

Section 8. The Secretary of the Treasury is hereby authorized and empowered to issue such further regulations as he may deem necessary to carry out the purposes of this order and to issue licenses thereunder, through such officers or agencies as he may designate, including licenses permitting the Federal reserve banks and member banks of the Federal Reserve System, in return for an equivalent amount of other coin, currency or credit, to deliver, earmark or hold in trust gold coin and bullion to or for persons showing the need for the same for any of the purposes specified in paragraphs (a), (c) and (d) of Section 2 of these regulations.

Section 9. Whoever willfully violates any provision of this Executive Order or of these regulations or of any rule, regulation or license issued thereunder may be fined not more than $10,000, or, if a natural person, may be imprisoned for not more than ten years, or both; and any officer, director, or agent of any corporation who knowingly participates in any such violation may be punished by a like fine, imprisonment, or both.

This order and these regulations may be modified or revoked at any time.

THE WHITE HOUSE
April 5, 1933.

FRANKLIN D ROOSEVELT

For Further Information Consult Your Local Bank

GOLD CERTIFICATES may be identified by the words "GOLD CERTIFICATE" appearing thereon. The serial number and the Treasury seal on the face of a GOLD CERTIFICATE are printed in YELLOW. Be careful not to confuse GOLD CERTIFICATES with other issues which are redeemable in gold but which are not GOLD CERTIFICATES. Federal Reserve Notes and United States Notes are "redeemable in gold" but are not "GOLD CERTIFICATES" and are not required to be surrendered

Special attention is directed to the exceptions allowed under Section 2 of the Executive Order

CRIMINAL PENALTIES FOR VIOLATION OF EXECUTIVE ORDER
$10,000 fine or 10 years imprisonment, or both, as provided in Section 9 of the order

W D Woodin
Secretary of the Treasury.

U.S. Government Printing Office: 1933 2-16064

OUR CURRENT REALITY: PAPER FIAT CURRENCY

"Neither paper currency nor deposits have value as commodities; intrinsically a 'dollar' bill is just a piece of paper."

—*Federal Reserve Bank of Chicago, 1975*

Paper fiat currency is an *extreme* form of debasing a currency. It is a currency that represents zero percent of any commodity (such as precious metals). It is not 90 percent nor is it 10 percent of any commodity. The only true natural value it has is the paper it is printed on. At times in history, people in various nations burned their fiat paper currency in stoves because it's true value was only to produce heat. *Our currency is fiat currency.* (We will discuss later why our fiat currency has any "value" at all) Throughout history, fiat currencies have *always failed.* Examples of fiat currency failures have been historically experienced in China (11th century), France (18th century), Germany (20th century), Argentina (20th century), Mexico (20th century), Zimbabwe (today), and the United States (18th century and today)! However, the truest and longest performing money substitute that has outlasted all fiat currency failures has been precious metals such as gold and silver. Due to the inevitable nature of government corruption, and ignorant government officials, fiat currency *has never and never will* keep its value anywhere near as well as gold and silver!

SUMMARY

". . .gold and economic freedom is inseparable."

—Alan Greenspan

Truth #2: Natural Law
Decides What Real Money Is
. . .Gold and Silver

- Sound Money has requirements set by natural law
- Gold and Silver meet these requirements
- Gold and Silver have been of value for *thousands* of years
- The American dollar has been of value for a little over 150 years
- Monetary Debasement —reduction of commodity base in currency
- Fiat Currency—no commodity base; no inherent value (what we have today)

CHAPTER THREE

INFLATION: THE SECRET WEALTH DESTROYER

"By this means, government may secretly and unobserved, confiscate the wealth of the people and not one man in a million will detect the theft."

—*John Maynard Keynes 1920 (Founder of Keynesian Economic Philosophy)*

So far we have learned that the best sound money is precious metals such as gold and silver. We have also learned that historical monetary debasement and fiat currencies have been unsuccessful in the end and have failed repeatedly. Gold and silver remain true money due to natural law. Precious metals have outlasted all the failed paper currencies of history and have roughly retained their unit of wealth. The question that we need to answer is *how* fiat currencies are so destructive not only to government and a country, but more importantly *to your investments*.

SHORT-TERM MEMORY: INFLATION'S EVIL ADVANTAGE

"Inflation hasn't ruined everything.
A dime can still be used as a screwdriver."

Ask yourself these questions:

Why did a hamburger in 1950 cost *only* 50 cents and now costs eight times that amount?

Why was the average annual salary in 1980 $15,000, compared to $40,000 in 2010 (2.5 times more)?

Why did a house cost $750 in 1913 and now costs about $150,000 in 2010 (200 times more)?

Fiat currencies *inevitably* cause inflation. This is because the government, which has control of the fiat currency, has many reasons why it prefers and supports inflation (we'll learn about those reasons later).

Inflation is the most underestimated economic concept in history.

It is so underestimated because it is a difficult subject for the average person to realize and understand. It is difficult for people to understand that, even though they have $100 now, in a year's time, it may only be worth the purchasing power of $97 of what it would have bought the previous year (even though it is still a $100 face-value dollar note). This concept sounds confusing at first. Inflation and its effects can be a subject that entails volumes of books. For our purposes, only the basic understanding is needed.

SIMPLE DEFINITION OF INFLATION

First, let's learn an important economic concept. As we stated before, there is a difference between the *nominal value* and the *real value* of something. Let's assume we are talking in terms of dollars. The nominal value is the number of dollars only. For example, fifty dollars is *lower* in nominal value when compared to one hundred dollars (50<100). This is what we learn in basic math class in school and why it is a major reason some people cannot fully understand the concept of inflation. Again, this is the nominal value. Unfortunately, the public has been lead to falsely believe that the nominal value is what determines wealth. It is understandable that people are led to believe this. People are good at simple math. If one person has $50,000 and another has $100,000, the person with the $100,000 is perceived to have more wealth. This is true. However, it is *very* important to acknowledge that we are referencing a nominal value of dollars, assumed to stay the *same* value over time. But that is not the case.

The *real value* is different than *nominal value.* And as we stated earlier, the nominal value may state an accurate difference in real value *only* if the underlying *real* value of the unit stays the same over time. Here's where the change occurs. If the nominal amounts are from different time periods, the real value may *not* be the same if the real value of the currency has fluctuated! The *real* value states how much purchasing power that nominal amount can purchase (or the wealth of the nominal amount). Purchasing power is what determines wealth. Because the value of our currency is not fixed and changes with time, the *real* value will change with time! For example, in 1910 $800 would have purchased a brand new house. Today, that $800 can maybe purchase one month's rent (depending upon circumstances). Even though the nominal value of the number 800 is the same, the *real* value is different. How and why does the real value change?

The *monetary supply* is the amount of currency in existence within an economic system. With paper fiat currency, the amount of currency can stay the same, decrease, or increase, because its amount can easily change. The amount is decided by whoever has the ability to control that currency (usually government and/or central bank).

Inflation is defined as an *expansion* or increase of the monetary supply. If more dollars are printed, the monetary supply increases. This is inflation. On the other hand, deflation is the opposite. Deflation is the *decrease* of the monetary supply.

Remember, that gold is *finite* and cannot be *printed* like the paper dollar. In regards to a gold standard, there is little, if any inflation or deflation, because gold's supply cannot be expanded or decreased significantly. The amount of money compared to the rest of the money supply in a gold standard will always stay relatively the same except for a small increase due to mining production, recycling, etc.

However, paper currency with no connections to a finite commodity that will act as a limit (such as gold) can be printed at the will of whoever has the printer. They just push the print button! *(So do you have the ability to print money? No…that's counterfeiting and you go to jail)*. This is how our money is inflated. It has been perpetually inflated over time. Inflation has a negative effect on the economy, especially *your savings and investments*. Here's why.

Inflation decreases the value of your savings. How do your savings decrease due to inflation? Well, that's simple. With your savings, you have a certain percentage, or cut, of the whole monetary supply that is in existence. If the person or entity who supplies the money decides to print more paper currency, your cut or percentage of the total monetary supply just got smaller. Your savings decrease by the action of the printer printing more money! It's a lot simpler than it sounds in words.

Because of inflation, there is a *second* negative effect. Not only do your savings decrease, but the *price of things you want to purchase increase. (How do the things you want to buy increase in price?)* If there is inflation, there is more "money" printed, which increases the monetary supply. After the money is used up by the special interests of government who get it first, the money finally finds its way into the pockets of average consumers like you and me (the economy). This gives the power for people to buy more products and services (because they have more newly printed currency). This seems good on the surface. Remember good intentions do not necessarily mean good outcomes. It is important to always look at the aftereffects of monetary policy. Don't forget the law of equality. The people who sell the products and services are also affected. People are now spending more money. If you're selling a product, why not *raise prices* since people have more money for your goods and services?

Rising prices are the second devastating effect of inflation (savings is the first). That is why in 1913 a house cost $750 and now it costs something more like $150,000! More dollars are in existence, so the person selling the house realizes he or she could sell it for a larger amount of currency. It would be crazy to sell a house for $750 today! The seller knows he or she can get more.

Let's say that in 1980, you saved $6,000 of your $15,000 average salary (40 percent of your income). Now fast forward to today in 2010. That $6,000 from

1980 cannot purchase the same amount of goods and services today! This is a loss of value of your savings! However, you have the same *nominal* value of dollars. Through monetary policy and faulty politics, more dollars have been pumped into the monetary system over time. Unfortunately, our government has accepted this Keynesian economic philosophy of having a steadily increasing monetary supply, which creates inflation. They think it is good! This has created inflation just about every year since our currency has been a fiat paper currency. Your hard-earned savings from a previous time are lost over time due to inflation. If inflation continues, eventually in the future a $200,000 annual salary will have the same meaning as a $30,000 annual salary today! And if you saved that $30,000 today, it will not nearly buy as much in the future!

Do you see how this has a negative effect on *your savings and purchasing power*? As we'll see later, it has an even greater effect on your investments! Inflation is the secret wealth destroyer and is *grossly underestimated*. Taxes which support government and seem to get many taxpayers angry, has nowhere near the ability to confiscate wealth from the citizens as inflation does. It's such a hard concept to understand, that people ignore its existence! However, the government knows fully well what it is doing. They need inflation to finance their debts and social government programs.

Zimbabwe 100 Trillion Dollar Note 2008

Woman burning currency for heat in Weimar
Republic after hyperinflation

WHY THE GOVERNMENT PREFERS INFLATION

"Inflation is taxation without legislation"

—Milton Friedman

When governments grow large they will *always* prefer inflation. In reality, large governments actually *need* it to survive. In order for governments to have grown large, they had to gain control of the currency. They took it away from the corrective gold standard, which would have made them default on their debt at a much earlier time. The United States would never had been able to sustain social security, Medicare, Medicaid, unemployment, welfare, and other social and financially unsustainable programs without the power of inflating the currency. The United States would have also gone bankrupt during the Civil War, both world wars, the Depression, the Vietnam War era, and every year since. There are many reasons why the government prefers inflation, as opposed to deflation, or even a steady purchasing power of the currency (such as a gold standard). The reasons for inflation are all advantageous to the government and destructive, as we learned previously, to its citizens (saver, purchaser, and investor). Here are some reasons why government prefers inflation:

1. *The government wants to lessen its debt.* In order to lessen the load of its unsustainable debt, it creates inflation. This makes the previous dollar amount of the debt worth less and easier to service. With inflation, it becomes much easier to pay back debt with newly-created money. It also reduces the debt of the federal government and the state and local governments. Large, oppressive government is the result. This creates dependency on inflation to support government programs. A perpetual inflationary philosophy becomes commonplace.

2. *It allows for massive government programs and buying of votes.* The increased debt load allows the government to pile on government social programs such as unemployment, welfare, Medicare, Medicaid, and other unsustainable social programs. Politicians will spend anything to get re-elected. When a large enough amount of people become dependent upon one or more of the programs, the politicians know they will secure the constituents' votes with the promise of more benefits. If there wasn't inflation, the country would quickly go bankrupt, due to these programs, and politicians would not be able to "buy" votes. People would be less dependent upon government and more dependent upon themselves, family, and community.

3. *Inflation helps failing businesses stay in business.* The debt that businesses attain is slowly reduced in time, regardless of whether or not they reduce the principle of the loan due to payments. Even if the business does not make enough of a profit to pay back its creditors, inflation will help reduce the value of the debt they incurred. This helps U.S. businesses last and makes them better able to compete with foreign companies. This is commonplace in corporate bond issues that have maturity lengths of many years. The creditors are the ones who lose and carry all the risk, while unsustainable businesses stay solvent.

4. *It increases real estate prices.* Real estate debt, the biggest form of debt and biggest current asset in the life of an average American, is reduced due to inflation. If inflation were not present, the current real estate crisis we are experiencing would be nothing compared to the severity it would be without inflation. People who could not afford to buy a house would foreclose. *(Now that's an idea!)* However, the government pushes for all people to be able to purchase homes. According to government, it is their "right." They insure loans through the FHA and HUD with cooperation from Fannie Mae and Freddie Mac. They issue the loans, even if the loans should not be made. The Federal government now insures more than half the homes in the United States

(insured essentially by the taxpayers). It severely distorts the economy.

5. *The government and Federal Reserve's stockpile of gold cannot be depleted.* If they need "money," they can easily push a button to print more paper fiat currency. They retain the *real wealth* (gold and silver which is the largest stockpile in the world) and demand that citizens use a depreciating currency, while the value of the gold increases over time. It does not matter that the best form of money is gold and silver. It could be something totally different, and they still will confiscate it and replace it with paper fiat.

6. *Power through special interests.* History has shown that government has always steered its course to obtaining more power over individuals. That is what unchecked government officials naturally do. Thomas Jefferson once said, "*The natural progression of things is for liberty to yield and government to gain ground.*" If the government can print money and give it directly to special interests, those special interests are the first to benefit from the newly-created currency. It is not until that newly created money is absorbed into the broad economy for price inflation to start having an effect on the broad economy. The special interests get to use the money before prices rise, when the new currency is at a higher

value. The power for government to fund special interests through newly-printed money is often underestimated in economics and politics.

These are just *some* of the reasons why government prefers inflation.

THE INFLATION VS. DEFLATION ARGUMENT

"If Americans ever allow banks to control the issue of their currency, first by inflation and then by deflation, the banks will deprive the people of all property, until their children will wake up homeless."

—*Thomas Jefferson*

It does not surprise me that there is a one-sided argument in the field of economics on inflation versus deflation. If you watch the financial news or access financial information from another source, you will most likely find that the commentators *always* state that inflation is better than deflation. They say that all measures, including inflation, should be taken to avoid deflation, because they associate it with so much negativity and fear. Well, let us see what inflation does.

Inflation

1. *Hurts Investors.* It decreases the return on investment and loans made by investors and creditors.
2. *Destroys Savings.*
3. *Erases and promotes more debt.* It does not matter if it is good or bad debt. However, bad debt is much more prevalent in a perpetual inflationary environment because inflation is expected.
4. *Larger Government* due to the increased social programs funded by inflation. We all know that more government control results in less individual liberty.
5. *Rising Prices* make it more expensive to buy goods and services. This has a devastating effect on the middle and poor classes of a country.

Inflation does not have good qualities. The only winners are government, which is in perpetual and infinite debt, its special interests, the Federal Reserve, and bad businesses. It promotes bad behavior. It destroys savings, hurts investors, creates larger tyrannical government, and increases the prices of consumer goods. Can you tell me again why on earth the financial commentators would suggest that inflation is a good thing? I think they are only looking at the *nominal* value and not the *real* value.

On the other hand, if there were deflation, the person who saved would be rewarded by a greater amount of purchasing power from his or her savings. It promotes saving. Once capital is saved and debt-related instruments are no longer prevalent in society, investment begins once again with real capital. Because money is increasing in value, it is advantageous to start a business that will have an increased income potential in order to receive *more* of the rising valued currency. These are just some of the positive effects of deflation. However, there are also many negative consequences of deflation just like there are with inflation.

The truth is that the inflation versus deflation argument is a fallacy. The inflation argument is heavily one-sided, due to the government and its dependents' need for inflation to support its debt and business dealings. The real answer is to have a currency that is *neither* inflationary nor deflationary. A stable currency produces a more efficient economy, because businesses can better predict the future. The stable currency does not create distorted economic conditions. A stable currency that results in both mild inflation and mild deflation results in a *sustainable and efficient* economy. It controls the growth of government and therefore sustains more individual liberty and prosperity. Again, we come to the best natural form of money, which are precious metals. Gold will not have the devastating effects of inflation or deflation.

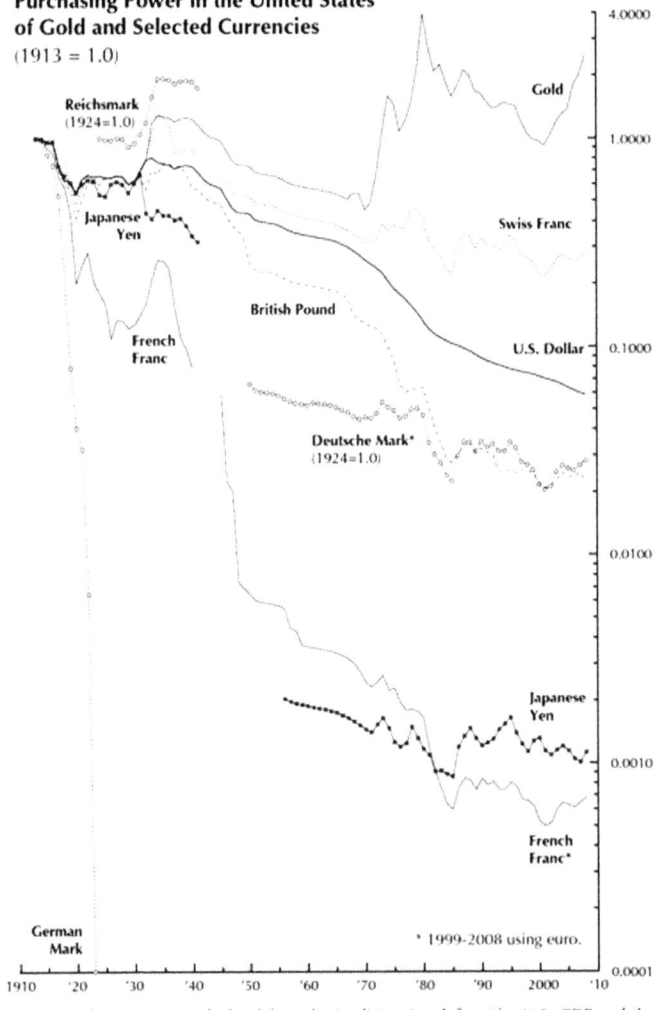

Purchasing Power in the United States of Gold and Selected Currencies
(1913 = 1.0)

Note: Purchasing power calculated from the implicit price deflator for U.S. GDP and the exchange rates of foreign currencies for U.S. dollars.

*FACT: THE U.S. DOLLAR HAS LOST …95 PERCENT OF ITS PURCHASING POWER SINCE 1913!
                    …89 percent since 1950!
                    …62 percent since 1980!
                    …21 percent since 2000!

Do you see how, over the long term, saving dollars in the bank is a *bad investment*?

Data is calculated to the year 2010. Data is retrieved from the Bureau of Labor Statistics.

SUMMARY

"In the absence of the gold standard, there is no way to protect savings from confiscation through inflation. There is no safe store of value."

—*Alan Greenspan, Former Federal Reserve Chairman*

Truth #3: Inflation Destroys Purchasing Power

- Inflation, which is the increase of the monetary supply, decreases the value of savings. It destroys wealth!
- Inflation also usually causes prices to rise (if there is a positive GDP).
- *The dollar is the worst investment!*. Saving money in the bank is a lost cause. The history of our fiat currency shows us that a loss of value is inevitable due to the nature of government's dependence on inflating the currency.

CHAPTER FOUR

THE FEDERAL RESERVE: AMERICA HIJACKED

*"Give me control of a nation's money
and I care not who makes its laws."*

—*Mayer Amschel Bauer Rothschild, English Banker*

The Federal Reserve may be the most dangerous act toward freedom in our country's history. That is a bold statement, but once you understand the amount of the loss of liberty that the Federal Reserve creates, you may agree with me. There is a small movement in America that understands and protests the existence of the Federal Reserve, but most Americans do not even know of its existence, let alone its expansive amount of absolute power. Almost all other threats to American liberty have been generally out in the open and, because of that awareness, are able to be defeated. However, the Federal Reserve bases itself upon secrecy and deception. It destroys the idea of America. It steals property from you and controls the outcomes of the economy.

The Federal Reserve is not "federal" in the sense that it is a government entity. It is often mistaken as such. The officials of the Federal Reserve are not elected by the people of our nation. There is no representation. It has very little ties to our government, yet has the *greatest* impact economically. *(Why do we give so much economic power to a private corporation?)* This is a question I ask myself constantly. It is the secrecy and deception that allow it to exist. If Americans really understood what was going on, like Henry Ford said, *"It is well enough that the people of the nation do not understand our banking system, for if they did, I believe there would be a revolution before tomorrow morning."* Again, there are numerous books on this subject alone. Here we are only skimming the basics so that we can apply them to our investments. So, what is the Federal Reserve and what impact does it have on *you and your investments*?

BRIEF HISTORY OF THE FEDERAL RESERVE

"Whoever controls the volume of money in any country is absolute master of all industry and commerce."
—James Garfield, U.S. President

The Federal Reserve, commonly nicknamed "The Fed," was created in *secret* in the early 20th century. Sounds like a conspiracy theory, right? Well it's not a theory. It's a fact. Historians acknowledge the secrecy of its birth. The men who constructed the Federal Reserve boarded a train form New York City to Georgia under the disguise of a friendly "bird hunt." They took with them shotguns to help disguise their intent. They told no one of their true intentions. Off the coast of Georgia in 1910, on a private island named Jekyll Island, this group of the most powerful and wealthiest bankers in the United States gathered, along with a few select government officials, and devised a plan to take control over the monetary system of the United States. They created the Federal Reserve. In order for it to be accepted by the citizens, it was masked through its deceiving title that appears as a government entity and the desire by the public for economic security during that time period. Also, the progressive (socialist) movement, which promoted tyrannical and socialist legislation, began in the early 20th century (like that of Woodrow Wilson and FDR). It was passed into law without much public attention in 1913. Now, our economy rests solely on its decisions.

Will it raise interest rates or will it lower them? Will it purchase government securities, or will it sell them? Will it purchase billions of dollars of mortgage backed securities to lower the impact of the housing crisis, and when will it decide to sell them? Will there be hyper-inflation, inflation, or deflation? Will mortgage rates be higher or lower in the future? Will the Federal Reserve fund international organizations and other foreign countries through the IMF with our currency, and which states and organizations will it choose to give that money to? Our day-to-day decisions are made *second* to the Federal Reserve's. Fortunes are made and lost depending on its decisions, which are only known to the Federal Reserve itself. When the Federal Reserve announces that it is raising interest rates, no one knows about it before hand. All of a sudden, your investments, savings, and purchasing power are effected by the decisions of a *few* men on the Federal Reserve Board of Governors. That is not liberty. That is tyranny. In my opinion, it's a criminal act, but that is for you to decide. But what does the Federal Reserve have to do with *you* and *your investments*?

DO NOT PASS GO: MONOPOLY MONEY

*"While boasting of our noble deeds, we're careful
to conceal the ugly fact that by an iniquitous money system,
we have nationalized a system of oppression which, though
more refined, is not less cruel than the old
system of chattel slavery."*

—Horace Greely

The Federal Reserve holds all the rights of creating our fiat paper currency. They are the printer. Take out a dollar bill from your wallet and look for yourself. Notice the paper bills in your wallet have the words "Federal Reserve Note" printed on the top face. This is *their* property. This was not always the case! Our currency used to be the property of the citizens, and the banks were private, with no connections to a central bank. If you look at the top left section of a dollar bill, you will notice the phrase, "This note is legal tender for all debts, public and private." What this really means is that the Federal Reserve, a private corporation not represented by the American people, has a *monopoly* on our currency. Even if the currency they produce is terrible, we still have to accept it by law.

Let us discuss this on the fundamentals of natural law. Suppose you were, by law, the only person allowed to produce automobiles. Do you think that the cars you produced would be of good quality? The answer is *no*. Here's why. People continually need to use cars (money in the Federal Reserve's case) for their daily living. If people are forced to buy and use the cars you manufacture under a *monopoly* and there is no competition from other car manufacturers, there is *no* incentive for you to improve and produce a high-quality product and lower the cost of the production. Your car (or currency in our case) deteriorates in quality. You'll get paid from selling cars at the price you choose, regardless of whether you produce a good quality car or a clunker! This is why business monopolies are considered illegal in the United States…but not for the Federal Reserve.

This monetary monopoly is dangerous for holders of paper dollars because the printing of additional paper dollars creates inflation and devalues the purchasing power of our savings. *Savings are destroyed.* The *only* reason why our fiat currency is worth *anything* is because we are forced to use it by law. If we were not forced to use it for public and private debts, the dollar would instantly become *worthless* with the application of competing currencies.

FRACTIONAL RESERVE BANKING SYSTEM: DEBT IS MONEY

"The few who understand the system, will either be so interested from its profits or so dependant on its favors, that there will be no opposition from that class."

—*Rothschild Brothers of London 1863*

It is important to understand the basic working of our banking system. The Federal Reserve and its member banks control the banking system. Not only is the currency under a monopoly by the Federal Reserve, but the entire banking system is also. There is much information about the current banking system of the Federal Reserve, but I just want to explain some important points that will help solidify your understanding of the current banking system. You will be surprised to find that money is not put into existence by labor, but by debt. *Money is debt*! A great way to understand the system is to follow the path it takes for our currency to get into your wallet.

1. Money is first printed by a department of the U.S. Treasury and then shipped over to the Federal Reserve. It is held there until the Federal Reserve *decides* to send it out into the economy. *(Inflation technically occurs here with the expansion of the monetary supply.)*

2. In order to send it out into the economy, the Federal Reserve "loans" money to its member banks at a low interest rate. The Federal Reserve only paid manufacturing costs for the currency, yet they are gaining interest on the loans given to its member banks at no expense or risk to themselves. In 2008 the Federal Reserve purchased 7.7 billion notes (not dollars) at 6.4 cents per note! *(They also make money on many other mischievous dealings, such*

as holding U.S. government debt that cost them nothing.)

3. The money is then lent out from the banks at higher interest rates to borrowers, such as businesses or individuals. The bank makes money off the spread from the Federal Reserve and the private loan. *(Also, in recessions, rising prices are sometimes suppressed because the banks do not loan out the money to individuals, but rather buy government debt to receive higher interest rates with "no risk." The money does not get out into the broad economy as easily.)*

4. The money that is loaned is now in the hands of the business or individual that received a loan from a member bank to use for their own purposes. *(This is where prices begin to rise and destroy savings, because the new money is spread out into the economy.)*

*When government takes out a loan and is given the money by the Federal Reserve, the government can bypass numbers 2 – 4 and give the money directly to their special interests. This allows the special interests to not be affected by rising prices and gives the government and special interests more power and wealth.

Another important aspect of banking is what is called fractional reserve banking. Fractional Reserve banking is specific to how the Federal Reserve banks operate. We have a fractional reserve banking system of nearly 90 percent. What does this mean? Here's an example. Let's say a Federal Reserve member bank issues a loan for $100,000. Ninety percent of that loan (which is really debt) is now considered an asset by the bank and can be re-loaned with newly printed money from the Federal Reserve. That loan is considered an asset and counts in the bookkeeping as part of the reserve requirement enforced by the Federal Reserve. Then 90 percent of the $90,000 of the second issued loan is considered an asset and can be re-loaned *again*. It's a snowball effect. Do you see how this could potentially become a problem, especially if those loans start to default? If you give out numerous loans (debt) to businesses or individuals, then you are creating a great amount of risk for yourself (the banks) because you don't have enough *true* capital assets compared to debt assets. Counting debt as your capital requirement is absurd, yet our banking system does just that. At the same time, it invites an inevitable loan crisis in the future, which then requires some sort of bailout or nationalization of the banks.

A typical argument would be that the bank holds a loan on a house, for example, and when a person defaults, they take ownership of the house and now have an asset. But as we have seen, we are living in a Keynesian-driven philosophy in our policies, government officials, and "top" economists. Keynesian economists allow for capital to enter an investment area to the point of extreme saturation. When all those houses start to default, the assets of the banks deteriorate at a massive rate. That is why, at the time of this printing, there are hundreds of banks being taken over by the Fed each year, since the housing crisis began, because they cannot survive. When a downturn in the fractional reserve banking system occurs, mass foreclosures and defaults are the result. Banks then need to be bailed out by the government and the Federal Reserve at the expense of the citizens. The Federal Reserve and government lose nothing. The citizens lose everything. In a free market, this would result in the complete failure of the bank. However, remember that the Federal Reserve and government, which control the banks and government debt, have the power to create as much money as they would like and bailout the banks at the public's expense. They can just print the losses! This rewards failure and distorts the free market. It has a significant effect on your property and investments.

INTEREST RATES: MORE ABSOLUTE CONTROL

"The accounts of the Federal Reserve System have never been audited. It operates outside the control of Congress and manipulates the credit of the United States."

—*Senator Barry Goldwater*

Along with the monopoly of our currency, we have also given the power to the Federal Reserve to control and set federal-fund interest rates. *(What are interest rates?)* If you take out any type of loan, you have an interest rate on which you pay *above and over* the principal that you borrowed. That extra money above the principal (called interest) is profit to whoever lent the money. For example, an annual 10 percent interest on a loan of $500, will give a profit of $50 per year to the lender in exchange for the risk he assumes for lending his own money. The profit protects the lender from possible defaults. It is profit for taking on risk.

In a *free market*, the interest rate is decided by supply and demand (natural law). For example, if a borrower does not have good credit history or the thing that the borrower is using the loan for has less of a chance to prove to be profitable, then the interest rate will need to be higher to account for the increased amount of *risk* the lender assumes. If there is a speculation bubble in a certain asset, people start to become concerned. The interest rate (in a free market) would rise to accommodate for that risk. During the housing bubble, the interest rates were lowered by force, which added more fuel to the fire and produced a worse outcome in the end.

The Federal Reserve has *almost complete* control over interest rates. It usually sets interest rates *below* the free market rate. This is due to their philosophy of having a constant period of inflation. Lower interest rates create "easy or cheap" money that people and businesses can access. Soon, there are investments in areas in the economy that are *not* economically sound and usually push it past the point in which a free market would have otherwise stopped it. This creates the *boom* of a great amount of loans being issued in unneeded areas of the economy. However, this also creates the inevitable bust. *Natural law always overcomes in the end*. When the economy becomes too saturated with the loans chasing inefficient areas of the economy, it crashes. A great example is the recent low interest rates of the 1990s through the 2000s, when the dot com era and housing bubble burst. If interest rates had been higher, therefore making it more expensive for people to borrow to buy houses, fewer people would have bought homes, because instead of interest rates at 6 percent, they might have been at 12 percent or 15 percent to accommodate the true market and its risks. The 12 percent interest rates or mortgages would have suppressed the excessive rise in housing prices by making it unaffordable for some people to buy. The fact is...THE FEDERAL RESERVE CREATES THE EXTREME BOOM AND BUST CYCLES AND PROLONGED DEPRESSIONS.

SUMMARY

"The [Federal Reserve Act] as it stands, seems to me to open the way to a vast inflation of the currency...I do not like to think that any law can be passed that will make it possible to submerge the gold standard in a flood of irredeemable paper currency."

—*Henry Cabot Lodge, Sr., 1913*

Truth #4: The Federal Reserve Controls Our Money System

- The Federal Reserve has a monopoly on our currency.
- The Federal Reserve has absolute power over interest rates, which should be set by the free market.
- The interest rate controlled by the Federal Reserve creates the extreme boom and bust cycles.

CHAPTER FIVE

STOCK MARKET GAIN

"I made a tremendous amount of money on real estate. I'll take real estate rather than go to Wall Street and get 2.8 percent. Forget about it."

—Ivana Trump

Previously, we discovered that holding our hard-earned dollars in the bank is *not saving*. The value of the dollar continues to decline, and our purchasing power is destroyed. It has a record of more than a 95 percent loss over the course of the past century. Like all fiat currencies in the past, it is a failed currency. Purchasing power loss is historically inevitable when a fiat paper currency is implemented. But don't we want dollars in order to purchase things? So, if holding dollars in a bank account or under the mattress is a *terrible* place to invest or even to try to store your wealth (95 percent loss), then where are we to turn?

The next avenue where many investors put their hard-earned money is in the stock market. How could you not? All the media outlets, investors, and "intellectuals" say that investing in the stock market is a great way to invest for the long term. Diversify, dollar-cost average, and wait. They say that short-term investing can be *risky* (and they are right). But, according to the "intelligent" investors, investing in the long term helps decrease the *risk*, while creating an often-touted historical return of 8 percent, 10 percent, or another percent they choose to elect in order to form a reason to invest long term. That high percent return sounds great…but wait. We learned about *inflation*, which decreases the value of the dollar almost every year. Remember, the stocks in the stock market are represented in a *dollar amount*, which is a *nominal* amount. So, if there is a gain in the stock market, there is also going to likely be a loss in real value, due to inflation at the same time. The media outlets, investors, and "intellectuals" say how much you gained in a year in *nominal* gain (dollar amount), but they often neglect to calculate the real value due to inflation (or purchasing power gain). I don't know about you, but if I have a large dollar amount gain, it doesn't mean anything significant if that increased amount of dollars cannot purchase a greater number of goods. It is a tricky and misleading concept. So, let us find what the stock market *really* gains each year, in inflation-adjusted terms, so that we can uncover the *real* long-term gain.

Here is how we calculate the return, using the government's inflation calculator:

To Find the *Nominal* Rate of Return
(The rate stated by media)

1. Find the dollar amount of both dates.
(Example: Year 1930: $20 Year 2010: $991)
2. Use a compound interest calculator *(http://www.moneychimp.com/calculator/compound_interest_calculator.htm)* to find the average annual return, for the first number to equal the second number over a specified number of years. This gives us the average annual return in reference to the dollar amount only. (The commonly stated return by "intellectuals")

(Example: The compound interest rate need in order to get from $20 to $991 over a 80 year time span would be 5%) Nominal Interest Rate = 5%

To Find the *Real* Rate of Return

1. Adjust the first date's number of dollars to equal the value of the underlying asset (dollar) in PRESENT-DAY DOLLARS. (Use BLS calculator)

http://www.bls.gov/data/inflation_calculator.htm
(Example: $20 from 1930 is the same as $262 in 2010 dollars due to inflation)

2. Redo the calculation with the compound interest calculator to find the inflation-adjusted, average annual return (the *real* return).

(Example: We substitute that $262 in place of the $20 and redo the calculation. We get a compounded interest rate of 1.54%. This shows us that the real rate of return is not 5% but rather 1.54%)

THE *REAL* STOCK MARKET

To analyze the *true* stock market gain, we need a time period to use as data. The Dow Jones Industrial Average began in 1896. I'm going to choose the time period of 1913 – 2010. I chose this time period for a few reasons. It is relatively long-term data. It also includes our own time that we live in plus 97 years back! The more important reason why I choose this time period is because the year 1913 is when the Federal Reserve came into existence. This is the birth year of the organization that controls the monetary supply and interest rates, which create inflation. This is important because this long-term data reflects the abuses from that organization. This is the period that will show the true value of investing in the stock market over the long term. This should be a long enough time period of data for those devoted to the mantra of long-term investing in the stock market. And I assure you that, if you started in 1900 or 1915, the results would come out relatively the same. I didn't pick the dates because they are most advantageous to my point. I only want to show *the real* return of the stock market over a long period of time. These results show the truth.

<u>Dow Jones Industrial Average 1913 – 2010</u>

1913
$87.8

2010
$10,428.05

Average Annual *Nominal* Gain: 5.05%
(In nominal terms/dollar amount gain)

If we purchased the Dow Jones Industrial Average (DJIA) in 1913 and held it until 2010, on the surface it appears there is a great amount of increase. The total value of those 30 stocks goes from $87.87 to $10,428. If you were to use a compounding interest calculator, you would find that it would calculate to an average annual gain of 5.05 percent. A 5.05 percent return sounds like a decent investment for some people. You would double your money in a little over 14 years. However, it isn't anything like the 10+ percent that investment companies or the media often advertise. Investment companies choose a smaller time period, which is more advantageous to their calculations in order to produce the famous 10+ percent average annual gain so that they can get people to invest which, in the end, makes their own company richer. But the *truth* is that it averages out to about 5.05 percent annually in nominal terms. But there is one very important economic factor that we still have to consider.

Let us not forget *inflation*! The amount of work it took to earn the $87.87 in 1913 was much greater than it is today to earn $87.87. The average annual salary was around a mere $750 per year! This means the dollar was worth *much more* in 1913! So, instead of the DJIA in 1913 being worth $87.87, let's find its *real* value in terms of *today's dollar*. If we convert the 1913 $87.87 dollar amount to what that amount would be in today's value and do the same calculation with a compound interest calculator, we will have an average inflation-adjusted return (or the *real* rate of return). To convert the dollar amount from 1913 to present day, we use the federal government's own Bureau of Labor Statistics (BLS) Inflation Calculator. According to the BLS inflation calculator, it will give us the true value of $87.87 in 2010. Let's calculate!

Dollar Conversion
$87.87 in 1913 = $1,923.26 in 2010 dollars!

Our next step in finding the annual inflation-adjusted return is to substitute the $87.87 in the previous calculation with $1,923.26. Again, we are going to use the compound interest calculator but, instead, we are going to use today's dollar value for 1913 ($1,923.26). We use the same calculation procedure, but instead, we use the adjusted dollar amount to inflation to give us a *real* return. The dollar conversion from $87.87 to $1,923.26 will obviously change the outcome of the calculation.

Dow Jones Industrial Average 1913 – 2010
(Inflation Adjusted)

1913
$1,923.26

2010
$10,428.05

Average Annual *Real Gain*: 1.76%
(In purchasing power gain)

Our calculation gives us an annual *real* return of 1.76 percent! This long-term investment does not seem so great anymore. The famous 10+ percent long-term gain in the stock market is actually only 1.76 percent when adjusted for inflation. What's the point of having a high return when the return is actually reduced because of the loss of purchasing power? Do you see how much inflation has an impact on your investments? Do you see how the media and investment companies fail to disclose the real inflation-adjusted rate of return? Throughout the next chapter, you will see this calculation done several times. I cannot stress the importance of including the purchasing power change of the dollar to the gains or losses in your investments. It is essential.

SUMMARY

Truth # 5: Stock Market Long-Term Return (1913 – 2010) is 1.76 percent

- Without recognizing inflation, the rate of return for our investment in the stock market over the long term is about 5.05 percent annual gain.
- The *inflation adjusted return* is only 1.76 percent!
- The stock market over the long term is *not a good investment*!

Economic Reality and Your Investments

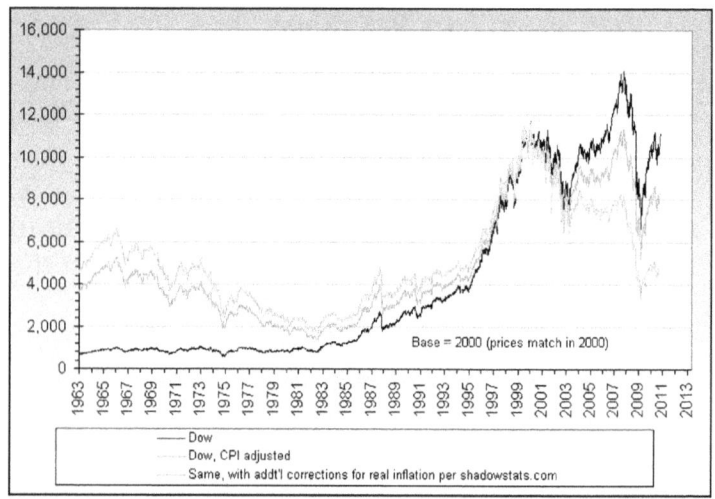

http://inflation.us/charts.html
This chart shows the DJIA in nominal, CPI adjusted, and Real Terms. It reveals that inflation has a significant impact of the real value of the stock market.

Chapter Five: Stock Market Gain

CHAPTER SIX

THE "GOLD BUG"

"More gold has been mined from the minds of men than has been taken from the earth."

—*Napoleon Hill*

If the stock market is not a good investment over the long term, then where can we invest our money? The contrary to investing in the stock market is often seen as investing in precious metals. Many wealthy people who realize and understand inflation swear upon investing in gold and silver. They know that gold has been of value for *thousands* of years. Also, different economies and countries have risen and fallen over time, yet the value of gold has endured. It sounds like a smart investment and in my opinion is better than the stock market. Let's see if putting our money in gold over the *same period of time* that we used for the stock market would have proved to be a better investment.

Gold 1913 – 2010

1913
$35

2010
$1,120

Average Annual *Nominal* Return: 4%

If you bought an ounce of gold in 1913 and held it until present day, it shows a substantial gain in the dollar amount. When using a compounding interest calculator to find the annual rate of return gold averages 4 percent annually in a nominal value. However, this is only the nominal gain and is neglecting inflation. What we need to do, just as we did with the DJIA to find the true long-term stock market gain, is to *adjust for inflation* because this price of gold is stated in a dollar amount. We all should remember what happens to the value of the dollar over time! By using the government's own inflation calculator, we can uncover the average inflation-adjusted return of gold.

Dollar Conversion
$35 in 1913 = $547.19 in 2010

Now we replace the 1913 dollar amount of $35 with $547.19 to convert it to today's dollar equivalent. Again, we use the compound interest calculator to calculate the average annual return.

Gold 1913 – 2010 *(Inflation Adjusted)*

1913
$35

2010
$1,120

Average Annual *Real* Return: .75%

At the writing of this book, gold has yielded an average real annual return of .75 percent when adjusted for inflation. Our conclusion is that the greatest money substitute (gold) may be a great way to store wealth over a long period of time, but is not a good way to invest over the long term if you want to increase your wealth. However, it has been a store of wealth for thousands of years, so it is more logical to own gold than invest in the stock market for the very long term since gold outlasts governments, economies, and currency changes. The returns of .75 percent of gold and 1.76 percent on the stock market are not anything close to great investments, yet these are common investment choices among common people for the long term. The people who promote either of these for substantial long-term gains are ridiculous! They do not disclose the *real* average inflation-adjusted return. What I want and I assume you do, too, is to invest to *make money*, and not just have your money keep its value!

SUMMARY

Truth #6: Gold's Long Term Average (Inflation Adjusted)
Return is .75%

- Without recognizing inflation, gold has had an annual compounded rate or return of 4 percent over the long term.
- The inflation-adjusted return is only .75 percent.
- Gold or precious metals are not good investments. However, they have been a store of wealth for thousands of years that have transcended governments and economies.

CHAPTER SEVEN

A SECRET PATTERN: UP-TREND AND CONSOLIDATION PERIODS

"In all chaos there is a cosmos, in all disorder a secret order."

—*Carl Jung*

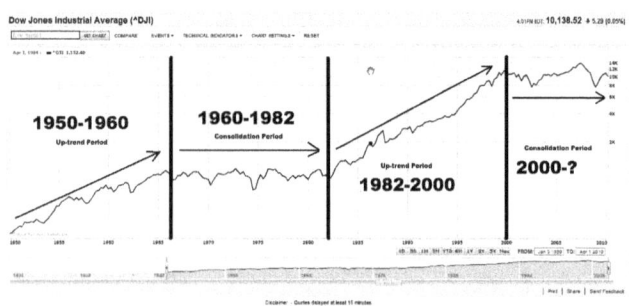

DJIA from 1950 – 2010
http://finance.yahoo.com/q?s=^DJI

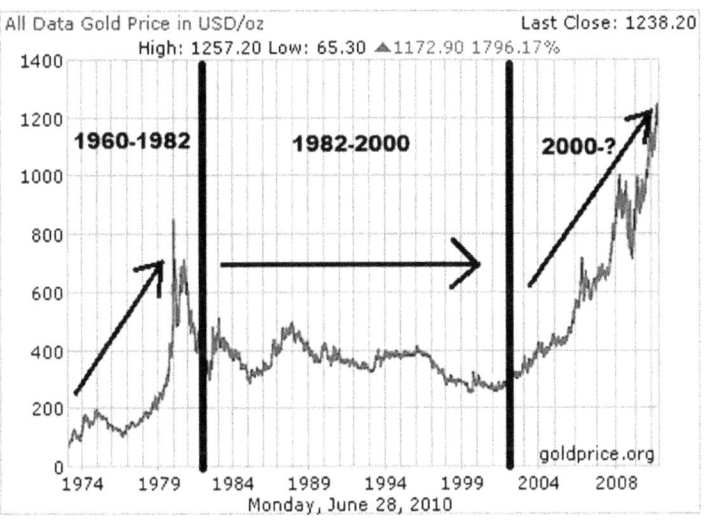

All Data Gold Price in USD/oz   Last Close: 1238.20
High: 1257.20 Low: 65.30 ▲1172.90 1796.17%

1960-1982   1982-2000   2000-?

goldprice.org

1974   1979   1984   1989   1994   1999   2004   2008

Monday, June 28, 2010

Gold 1950 – 2010

In this section, you will learn the secret to how rich investors make their money. They don't risk their money on one stock (unless it's insider trading, which is illegal). The rich don't invest in CDs or invest for the "long term." You are about to learn their investing secret. It uses all of the previous material that you have read, including the history of money, inflation, and the Federal Reserve. It all gets wrapped up into one historically sound and logical idea. This is how the *rich* invest.

Most people enjoy a life of independent income from approximately age twenty to age sixty-five. That is a total of forty-five years. The average life expectancy for the American citizen is seventy-eight years. Let's say that from age twenty to age seventy-eight, you are financially independent in the sense of "being on your own." This gives you fifty-eight years of having to do something with the money that you earn. Some goes to living expenses and other expenditures. The other portion will go to "savings" or investments. So any investment strategies that include investment calculations that are more than fifty-eight years in length are really not applicable to one's own life. Even investment strategies taken data from lengths of time of more than twenty-five years is not practicable, because I'm sure that, if you are twenty years old, you wouldn't want to wait a quarter century to see your investments rebound if there was a downturn in your assets. Investing for the "long term" that everyone says is a great idea isn't that practical in perspective to your own life to begin with. It is good to acknowledge the broad historical examples of economies and the foundation of money, but unless you can figure out how to live for centuries, it is unwise to calculate risks and rewards on such a time scale.

Let me entertain you on shorter periods of time that will better apply to your life, but not too short that there is a great amount of risk (anything can happen to the stock market or gold over only a few years time). Let me show you some specific time periods of investments that will take your breath away. They are called up-trend periods (when the stock market goes up and gold goes down) and consolidation periods (when the stock market remains flat and gold goes up). This can be easily seen in the previous two charts. These charts are important and should be a common reference to the reader. The reader should also notice the trends in these charts. We will use the same method as in the previous chapter to calculate the *inflation adjusted returns* of these individual periods.

1950 – 1966 (SIXTEEN YEARS) *UP-TREND*

<u>DJIA 1950 – 1966</u>

1950
$200.52

1966
$969.26

Results of calculation:

DJIA Annual Average *Nominal* Return: 10.35%

As you can see in the previous graph of the DJIA 1950 – 1966, there is an obvious up-trend period of the stock market. If we calculate the average compounded return *without* adjusting for inflation, we find it to be an average of 10.35 percent gain per year in nominal terms. However, we need to find the inflation adjusted return to realize what we truthfully receive as a return in terms of purchasing power.

Dollar Conversion

$200.52 in 1950 = $269.55 in 1966

<u>DJIA 1950 – 1966 *(Inflation Adjusted)*</u>
1950
$269.55

1966
$969.26

Results of Calculation:

DJIA Average Annual *Real Return*: 8.33%

Here we find that we have a *real* return of 8.33 percent. That is still a good return in terms of purchasing power! I'm curious if gold fared as well during the same time period. However, there is one fact that we need to keep in mind. The gold standard for foreign payments was still in place during this time period. Gold remained relatively the same value through this specific time period, up until 1971 when the foreign gold standard was broken. But let's check it out anyway.

<u>Gold 1950 – 1966</u>

1950
$34.72

1966
$35.13

Results of calculation:

Gold Annual Average *Nominal* Return: .07%

In nominal terms, gold's has stayed the same. Let us find out what the *real* return is in terms of purchasing power.

Dollar Conversion
$34.72 in 1950 = $46.68 in 1966

Gold 1950 – 1966 *(Inflation Adjusted)*

1950
$46.68

1966
$35.13

Results of calculation:

Gold Average Annual Inflation Adjusted Return:
-1.76%

CONCLUSION: 1950 – 1966
REAL RETURNS

Stock Market: 8.33% *(*10.35%)*
Gold: -1.76% *(.*07%)*

*Non-Inflation-Adjusted Return

1966 – 1982 (SIXTEEN YEARS)
CONSOLIDATION

<u>DJIA 1966 – 1982</u>
1966
$969.26

1982
$875

Results of Calculation:

DJIA Average Annual *Nominal* Return: -.63%

Dollar Conversion
$969.26 in 1966 = $2,886.84 in 1982

DJIA 1966 – 1982 (*Inflation Adjusted*)
1966
$2,886.84

1982
$875

Results of Calculation:
DJIA Average Annual *Real* Return: -7.18%

The stock market did terrible in terms of purchasing power! This terrible investment period was not just a year or two, as is usually perceived in a recession or depression, but in the span of sixteen years! The stock market was stuck in a consolidation period for sixteen years, while inflation ate away at the purchasing power of the value of stocks. I definitely would not want to have invested in stocks during this period. Inflation must have been very high during that time to reduce that return from -.63 percent to -7.18 percent! What about gold?

Gold 1966 – 1982
1966
$35.13

1982
$376
Results of Calculation:

Gold Average Annual Nominal Return: 16%

Wow! That's outstanding! However, inflation seemed to be high during this period, as we saw with the *real* return of the stock market. What about the inflation-adjusted return of gold?

Dollar Conversion
$35.13 in 1966 = $104.63 in 1982

Gold 1966 – 1982 *(Inflation Adjusted)*

1966
$104.63

1982
$376

Results of calculation:

Gold Average Annual *Real* Return: 8.32%

CONCLUSION: 1966 – 1982
AVERAGE REAL RETURNS

Stock Market: -7.18% *(-.63%)*
Gold: 8.32% *(16%)*

Non-Inflation-Adjusted Return

1982 – 2000 (SEVENTEEN YEARS)
UP-TREND

DJIA 1982 – 2000

1982
$875

2000
$11,497.12

Results of calculation:

DJIA Average Annual *Nominal* Return: 16.36%

Wow! A 16 percent return is outstanding! But once again, let us compensate for inflation.

Dollar Conversion
$875 in 1982 = $1,561.40 in 2000

DJIA 1982 – 2000 *(Inflation Adjusted)*

1982
$1,561.40

2000
$11,497.12
Results of calculation:

DJIA Average Annual *Real* Return: 12.47%

Gold 1982 – 2000

1982
$376

2000
$279.11

Results of calculation:

Gold Average Annual *Nominal* Return: -1.73%

Dollar Conversion
$376 in 1982 = $670.96 in 2000

Gold 1982 – 2000 *(Inflation Adjusted)*

1982
$670.96

2000
$279.11

Gold Average Annual *Real* Return: -5.03%

CONCLUSION: 1982 – 2000
AVERAGE REAL RETURNS

Stock Market: 12.47% *(16.6 %*)*

Gold: -5.03% *(-1.73 %*)*

*Non-inflation-adjusted return

I would have rather invested in the stock market! This keeps going back and forth. *(Is there a pattern here?)* Gathering information from the previous calculations, what do you think will happen during the following years after 2000? Let's see!

2000 – 2010(PRESENT)

(TEN-PLUS YEARS) *CONSOLIDATION*

DJIA 2000 - Present

2000
$11,497.12

2010
$10,428.05

Results of calculation:

DJIA Average Annual *Nominal* Return: -.97%

Dollar Conversion:
$11,497.12 in 2000 = $14,467.34 in 2010

DJIA 2000 – Present *(Inflation Adjusted)*

2000
$14,467.34

2010
$10,428.05

DJIA Average Annual *Real* Return: -3.22%

Gold 2000 – Present

Gold 2000
$279.11

Gold 2010
$1,120

Gold Average Annual *Nominal* Return: 14.91%

Dollar Conversion:
$279.11 in 2000 = $351.22 in 2010

Gold 2000 – Present *(Inflation Adjusted)*

2000
$351.22

2010
$1,120

Gold Average Annual *Real* Return: 11.25%

SUMMARY

Truth #7: Gold and the Stock Market Alternate Periods of Real Gains (due to the effects of inflation)

INFLATION-ADJUSTED REAL RETURNS

1950 – 1966

DJIA: +8.33 percent per year (*10.35 percent)
Gold: -1.76 percent per year (.*07 percent)

1966 – 1982

DJIA: -7.18 percent per year (*-.63 percent per year)
Gold: +8.32 percent per year (*16 percent per year)

1982 – 2000

DJIA: +12.47 percent per year (*16.36 percent)
Gold: -5.03 percent per year (*-1.73 percent)

2000 – 2010

DJIA: -3.22 percent per year (*-.97 percent)
Gold: +11.25 percent per year (*14.91 percent)

* NON-Inflation-Adjusted Return

Chapter Seven: A Secret Pattern: Up-trend and Consolidation Periods

CHAPTER EIGHT

THE SECRET KEY TO INVESTING

"I want to be with those who know secret things or else alone."

—*Rainer Maria Rilke*

Finally, you have reached the part that most readers have been waiting for. This is the way rich people invest. Throughout the book, we have learned the history of money and the Federal Reserve, economic concepts such as inflation, and distinct alternating time periods of up-trends and consolidations of the stock market that run opposite to gold. The stock market and gold switch places as being the best investment during alternating time periods, as we have seen in the previous chapter. The time period that we are in now (2010) is a period where gold is the greatest investment and the stock market is one of the worst. One day, it will change once again to where gold is a terrible investment and the stock market is yet again "king". We know the time periods are real because there is historical evidence, the Federal Reserve actions, and inflationary policies.

But the next question is how does a person make the timely decision to transition from one period into the next?

The trends are easy to see. However, no one can pinpoint the exact time of change. Remember, there is risk to any type of investment (including savings). But, we can use data that gives us a good idea. The way the time periods are timed refers back to natural fundamentals about inflation and the economy. Look at the following chart of the S&P P/E Ration.

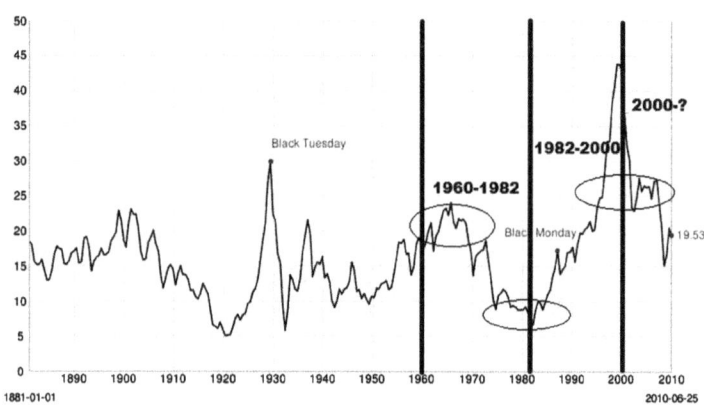

S&P 500 P/E Ratio (10 Year Trailing)
Data courtesy of Robert Shiller,
Yale Department of Economics
http://www.multpl.com

This is a chart of the twelve-month trailing S&P 500 P/E ratio. That sounds like another confusing economic term! Let's take it step by step. The DJIA is a group of thirty companies. The S&P 500 consists of (you guessed it) 500 different stocks. Scientists know that when there is a bigger testing pool, you get more accurate results. This is why I use the data of 500 stocks so that one stock does not have a significant impact negatively or positively on the whole data.

The "P" of the ratio stands for price. All of the 500 stocks prices put together is the price. The "E" stands for earnings. "Earnings" are how much the 500 stocks make in profit. The P/E ratio is the simple equation of price divided by earnings, which gives you the ratio number! For example, let's say hypothetically that the price is

$100. The earnings happen to be $10. The P/E ratio would be 10 (100/10 = 10)! Now if it was $200 and they still had only $10 in earnings, the P/E ratio would be 20 (200/10 = 20). Notice how the price of the stocks went up, but the earnings stayed the same. Thus, the P/E ratio rose to a higher number. This means that the stocks are more overvalued or more overbought. People are paying more for them at the higher P/E ratio! Therefore, it would be wise for you to buy stocks when the S&P 500 P/E ratio is low and sell your stocks when it is high. It's that simple!

As you can see in the chart, the S&P 500 P/E ratio goes up and down over the same time periods that we saw before! One time period length goes from roughly 10 to a high of 22. When the P/E ratio is at 10, the stocks are undervalued and are a good deal (on sale)! When the P/E ratio is above 20, the stock market is overbought! If you take a time period where the P/E ratio begins at 10 and ends at 22, you will notice that, during that time period, the stock market rose! Those are the same periods in which we found the stock market to gain and gold to lose!

The subsequent time period of the P/E ratio begins at 22 and ends at 10. Here, the stock market goes down, and gold goes up! Just like our data earlier! So here it is! We invest in stocks when the P/E ratio is near 10, and invest in gold when the P/E ratio is near 22. It's that easy!

One thing to remember is that the time periods usually last from around fourteen to seventeen years.

So if the P/E ratio says to change, but the time period is not near those many years, then it is a false signal and should be ignored. False signals can happen due to abnormal circumstances. But remember inflation has not yet run its course on the value of the asset.

SUMMARY

Truth #8: The Periods of Gold vs. Stock Market Can Be Timed

How to Invest

Time periods of fourteen to seventeen years.
Near P/E ratio 10, investments heavier in stocks.
Near P/E ratio 22, investments heavier in gold.

So easy! So why does this work so well?

CHAPTER NINE

WHY IT WORKS

"Order and simplification are the first steps toward the mastery of a subject."

—*Thomas Mann*

As stated previously, it is very important not to just know the name of an investment, but to also know why it works so well. Look deeper into how this particular investment has been successful for many lifetimes. There are three fundamental reasons why it works.

1) Basic Economic Fundamentals
2) Current Monetary Policy
3) Historical Proof

In each of these, there are many smaller individual reasons why this investment works. You have already learned about many of them. Let us gather all that has been learned into a summary perspective. In this part of the book, we will get a better overall understanding of why it works. .

BASIC ECONOMIC
FUNDAMENTALS: INFLATION

"Gold is not necessary. I have no interest in gold. We will build a solid state, without an ounce of gold behind it."
—*Adolf Hitler*

Inflation is a key factor to the validity of this investment. If you do not understand the concept of inflation, you will not appreciate and understand how this investment works. Protection against inflation is protecting against the loss of purchasing power of an otherwise seemingly steady nominal amount of dollars. As stated previously, government enjoys all the benefits of inflation, while the citizens are misled, and their savings and investments are severely damaged over time. Although it may not be necessary to understand inflation in order to follow the investment guidelines, it will give you a much better understanding of what you are investing in and give you more confidence through the shorter time periods of volatility that will test your commitment. It is never a good idea to invest in something that you don't understand (like the mortgage securities of the late 2000s). Inflation affects many things, such as your savings, investments, goods and services, size of government, and many other intended and unintended consequences. So far, our government and Federal Reserve have followed the Keynesian philosophy. We have a gradual and perpetual inflationary policy in force with raging bouts of high inflation. I do not see that changing. The amount of current government debt and future unfunded liabilities need to be reduced through inflation in order for the American economic power to continue. The government could raise taxes to 100 percent and *still* not be able to pay for government debt and obligations. They will *need* to try to inflate the currency to pay for it with newly created dollars. If we do not inflate our currency, we will surely go into technical default. This will be the government's last resort. Inflation is one of the major reasons this concept works and it's a fact.

Inflation consistently devalues our currency. When the stock market is in an up-trend period, an economic expansion is occurring. Business booms as a result of the easy credit of artificially low interest rates. As always, people get too excited, and the stock prices become higher than their true value. There's a point where natural markets just can't take it anymore. Business stops and a consolidation period is the result. Although the nominal stock market price does not go up or down during the consolidation period, the purchasing power is reduced. Real wealth is destroyed. Investment companies get away with telling their clients that they haven't lost any dollars in nominal terms over the consolidation period. It's true. But have they lost *any real* wealth? You bet.

[See DJIA Chart 1966 – 1982]
page 97

During this consolidation period, inflation runs its course. At the same time, it decreases the purchasing power of your savings, because more money is in the economy. Due to this influx of dollars products become more expensive. The businesses begin to make higher earnings over time. Remember the P/E ratio? If earnings go up, then the ratio decreases. This allows for inflation, over time, in the consolidation period, to decrease the P/E ratio of the stocks to a cheaper *real* price. This allows stocks to again become more affordable. Then the process starts all over again.

CURRENT MONETARY POLICY: THE FEDERAL RESERVE

"From now on, depressions will be scientifically created."

—*Congressman Charles Lindbergh, Sr., 1913*

As we learned earlier, the Federal Reserve controls interest rates, which distort true interest rates that would otherwise be regulated by the free market. The seizure of this free market principle by the Federal Reserve ultimately creates the extreme "boom and bust" cycle we know today by not allowing corrections when the market asks for it, thus extending periods of economic expansions and setting up the inevitable bust. Long periods of economic expansion or easy credit (our fifteen-year up-trend period) is instantly followed by a relatively equal downturn (fifteen-year consolidation period). The interest rates encourage and exaggerate this cycle to make it obvious and predictable. The only good thing that comes from the Federal Reserve is our ability to understand their motivations and how to invest wisely. Unfortunately, many people will not read this book and, if they do, will reject it as being "unwise" because it goes against popular belief. Most people will be victims while others will be beneficiaries.

HISTORICAL PROOF

There has been more than enough historical proof that this investment strategy works. It has worked for nearly seventy years and can be easily seen by viewing a few simple charts (DJIA, Gold, S&P 500 P/E Ratio). The reason why it has not worked for more than this amount of time is because there was, at one time, a gold standard. The domestic gold standard ended in the early 1900s. However, there was still a foreign exchange gold standard. This was ended in 1971. Because of the actions of the Federal Reserve and the relatively recent abolishment of sound money during the twentieth century, this investment strategy cannot be assumed to be accurate before this time period, when the gold standard was in force. Inflationary policies did not have an impact like they do today. But who has an investment strategy that dates back to the 1800s anyway? Most investment strategies are based on less than a quarter century, while this is based on a century of time (and more, considering natural law and sound money). I don't know what else to tell you as a reader of this book about the historical accuracy. The time periods stand out and make a bold statement. The government and the Federal Reserve have perpetually inflated the currency. Many will try to come up with "intellectual arguments" against the historical accuracy of this data.

CONCLUSION

There are many reasons why this investment works. The reasons stated in this book are the most important reasons. However, if you choose to study further, you will find even more evidence that supports this investment. Now that you know *why* and *how* it works, it is an investment that you can participate in!

Chapter Nine: Why It Works

WHY PEOPLE WILL REJECT IT

"People will generally accept facts as the truth only if the facts agree with what they already believe."

—*Andy Rooney*

This investment theory is supported by historical facts, current monetary policy, and fundamental economics. To reject that and, instead, accept the widespread belief that the dollar is a store of value is insanity. It is absolute truth that the dollar has lost 95 percent of its value over a century. Even the government, which I have little faith in today, states the extreme loss of purchasing power of the dollar on the U.S. Bureau of Labor Statistics website. The facts do not lie, no matter how much the media, investment firms, politicians, or *your own mind* try to reject them. There will be many people who will continue to follow destructive investment practices. Even some people that read this book will find that their minds cannot accept the truths and will find that excuses will build up until they force themselves to follow the crowd. There are many reasons, most of which are emotional and subconscious, which will turn people away from the truth.

I also tried to reject many of the facts stated in this book when I began my research. Popular belief blinds logic and censures much of the truth from many people. It is said that insanity is continually doing the same thing and expecting different results. Yet, once again, as mankind we are repeating the same mistakes that history has already experienced. It is through generational time gaps, the expectation that things will continue as they have no matter what, and basic human psychological tendencies that we will repeat our past mistakes. Socialism does not work. Yet, we will try it again. Inflation and debt do not work. Yet, we will try it again. If you look at history, you can easily argue that we, as a human race, are technically insane. This book is written to help reveal the truth and turn you away from that insanity in regards to your investments.

UNDERSTANDING THE EFFECTS OF INFLATION

"Truth will always be truth, regardless of lack of understanding, disbelief, or ignorance."

—W. Clement Stone

Inflation is a complicated economic concept. How do you explain that, when you receive a high return on an investment in a nominal dollar amount, the value of the dollar depreciates at the same time? It's complicated for people to get their minds around that concept. It's even harder to consider the destructive effect that it has on investments and savings. It's hard for the average person who always held confidence in the dollar, when in reality the dollar's purchasing power has steadily decreased in real value. The failure of realizing the dollar's deficiencies as a place to store wealth has been the reason why people continue to insist on putting money in the bank when, in fact, it is not saving at all. This is the biggest factor why people will reject the idea of the secret investment. If you understand inflation and the effect of inflation on your money and investments, then you have a distinct advantage over the rest of the population.

FAITH IN GOVERNMENT

"None are more hopelessly enslaved than those who falsely believe they are free."

—Johann Wolfgang Von Goethe

We live in a great country. I would not want to live any place else. Our country is great because of the foundation that was set forth by people like Samuel Adams, George Washington, Benjamin Franklin, Thomas Jefferson, and many others. It is a foundation of liberty. Their focus was not on government, but on the individual rights of each person.

However, our government has changed. It is not truly American in the original sense. Our government today has disguised itself as being a country of "freedom," "justice," "equality," and other rights. It has even touted that we are a "democracy" when we are not. We are a Republic. There is a great difference. The government uses these terms from the previous generations of government that actually practiced this. It does this in order to deceive the general population into accepting socialistic programs and laws.

Over time, people have gained so much faith in government that it has become a blind faith. Our politicians have taken advantage of that. Even the people who speak out against big government control still find comfort in holding a paper dollar, which the government and the Federal Reserve control. The fact is that there is a monopoly on the currency by a private organization that has destroyed the currency for its benefit and the benefit of a large oppressive government. Past history of our country as being a beacon of freedom many years ago, has given the false perception that the United States will always be just and trustworthy. However, in reality, it is not the government that is just, but the people who hopefully will correct that danger-ous path in the not too distant future. Big governments always lead to corruption, but people have trusted that government has done what is best for the general population. That is not the truth, yet countless people will reject any statement of corruption by their beloved "government" which they mistake for their country.

"YOU CAN'T EAT GOLD"

"It is always better to have no ideas than false ones; to believe nothing, than to believe what is wrong."

—*Thomas Jefferson*

This is a common thought by people who refuse to accept the truth that the best form of money that adheres to natural law is precious metals such as gold. This truth has been backed by the fact that gold has been the dominant form of money for the *longest* time throughout history. It has endured for thousands of years. It has survived changes of governments and cur-rency collapses.

Obviously, it is true that you cannot eat gold. However, I find it hilarious when people make this argu-ment. Can a person eat stocks, bonds, or our paper dol-lar? Due to brainwashing, people *still* reject the idea of gold being money. Often, people think of gold as only being valuable in an extremely depressed economic environment. They come to this conclusion because, when the stock market is in a consolidation period (or stagnant/depressed economic environment), gold rises as it combats inflation of the paper dollar. When referring to not being able to eat gold, people are thinking of such an extremely broken economic system where we return to a barter economy. Gold has been money regardless of an economic collapse or not. Throughout economic expansion and depression, gold has *still* been money. In order for gold to be money, people often think of an economic collapse where they see people kill other people for food, mass exoduses of major cities, and no cars driving on the roads. If that does happen, we will no longer be using dollars, and stocks will be worthless. And, most likely, gold will have little value as well. I don't believe that we will return to a barter economy, because there is too much trade infrastructure. And if we were to have a complete economic and social collapse, people don't stop exchanging goods. An economic collapse will demand the currency to return to a sound form of money which is gold. Trading will quickly resume shortly thereafter. If you study past economic collapses in other countries, gold still holds its value and rises during those periods, while at the same time, the currency and businesses are destroyed. But, natural law does not demand for an economic collapse in order for gold to be of value. I would rather have my faith in gold, which has held its real value for *thousands of years* through all economic booms and busts, than in a paper fiat currency with a current lifespan of only one hundred, fifty-plus years and has in fact lost over 95 percent of its value in one century.

STOCKS ARE ALWAYS BETTER THAN GOLD

"Stocks have reached what looks like a permanently high plateau."

—*Irving Fisher, University of Yale Economic Professor, 1929 (right before the great depression)*

The largest U.S. businesses survive forty years on average. The smaller businesses' life span is even shorter. I'm not sure about you, but I don't want to invest in anything that can die all of a sudden and has that short of an average life span! What happens if I pick the wrong one? The death and birth of business is normal and healthy. This mimics nature (and rightly so). Yet investors still invest large portions of their portfolios in just a few companies that they think will increase (a.k.a. gambling). They feel foolish *after* the company fails (Enron, Freddie Mac, LTCM, Circuit City, etc.). It can happen for any number of unforeseen reasons, such as technology advancement, consumer demand, outsourcing, bad management, broad-market movements, accounting corruption, etc. Why on earth would anyone take that chance on one company?

It is funny when I mention the previous concept to people. Their initial response is, *"Well, you diversify for the long term."* I have no problem with diversification. I think it is a smart way to invest. However, we all know what the overall market does over the long term. If you are happy with the one-percent gain and the stock market roller-coaster you need to ride emotionally for fifteen-year periods in the meantime, then be my guest! But I'd rather make 10 percent *above* inflation on average each year! At the same time, no one knows the short-term future of a year or so. This makes short-term investing even more risky. Also, taxes are usually higher for short-term investments, which will further decrease the investment return.

It is obvious that stocks are not necessarily going to always be better than gold. That is what this book illustrates. There are times when it is. But there are time periods of approximately fifteen years when stocks are terrible investments. This widely-held belief that stocks are the best investment is fallacious and is widely propagated by the financial industry.

LACK OF PERSONAL EXPERIENCE: GENERATIONAL TIME GAP & GEOGRAPHICAL DISLOCATIONS

As is the generation of leaves, so is that of humanity.
The wind scatters the leaves on the ground, but the live timber
Burgeons with leaves again in the season of spring returning.
So one generation of men will grow while another dies.

—*Homer, Iliad*

As stated before, it can be argued that mankind is technically insane. Over long periods of time, we do the same things while expecting different results. With generational time gaps, people do not get to experience first hand the effects of certain actions and results. This lack of experience allows us to underestimate actions and expect different results.

Let's go back in time for a moment. Transfer yourself back to 1923 in Germany, right after they inflated the currency so its value became nothing. I guarantee that 99 percent of the citizens would have expressed to you very emotionally that you should not trust the government's currency, especially if it was a fiat currency. They would have made such an emotional case for you to own gold, rather than the Reishmark, that you would have been sold by their enthusiasm. It is their personal experience that would have changed your mind. We lack that.

Fidel Castro's Cuban communist revolution happened relatively recently in our history. Cuba used to be the place for Americans to visit. It was almost like the Las Vegas or Cancun that we enjoy as a vacation destination today. After the communist revolution, things dramatically changed. The socialist actions forced by the government destroyed much of their economy and left the country in extreme poverty. The old 1950 American cars that still are seen driving on the roads show the remnants of the prosperous past. It is not for luxury or nostalgia that they still drive these cars. Rather, it is that they cannot afford to buy any new cars because they are too poor. They must service the existing cars to get them to run as long as possible; even if they are from 1950. If you ask any Cuban-American today that personally experienced the communist revolution, they will tell you the horrible effect of the revolution. They will speak of murder, poverty, and the lack of freedom. Yet, we have young people in our country wearing Ché Guevara T-shirts, a top leader of the communist revolution in Cuba that killed hundreds of people. They do it because it's cool and their own ignorance. It is the equivalent of wearing a shirt with Adolf Hitler's face on the front. Here's the bottom line. People *die* trying to float to the United States on makeshift rafts each year. So, why are not Americans dying trying to go to Cuba?

As citizens, we sit complacently when our oppressive government is passing socialistic programs and laws. It is because we have never personally experienced socialism like in Cuba, Russia, or any other communist regime. We do not understand the effects of hyperinflation like the people of Zimbabwe do today, because we are geographically disconnected. We don't have the personal experience. This is why many will reject the truth.

"IT'S TOO EASY"

"The great seal of truth is simplicity."

—Herman Boerhaave

Some people will reject it because they feel as if it is too easy. Some failing investors believe that you need to understand and implement complicated and confusing investment vehicles and strategies in order to receive a higher return. They believe foreign investment terms (like mortgage-backed securities) result in prosperity on the sole fact that it is complex. However, the fact is that the more complexity there is, the greater the chance of corruption. Fundamentals and the law of nature do not yield to man's attempts at manipulation. Man constructs things from nature. You cannot change nature. These are the same people who thought that the housing sector would *never* crash and that mortgage-backed securities, which they knew nothing about fundamentally, were great investments. The facts in this book are simple, but some people subconsciously will always reject the truth for whatever reason they justify as being acceptable to their false beliefs. These are the people who struggle financially with their investments.

Chapter Ten: Why People Will Reject It

YOUR INVESTMENT PORTFOLIO

An investment in knowledge pays the best interest.

—*Benjamin Franklin*

THE SECRET INVESTMENT: IN A NUTSHELL

"Men occasionally stumble over the truth, but most of them pick themselves up and hurry off as if nothing ever happened."

—*Winston Churchill*

So there you have it: economic reality and the secret key to your investments. It is a simple strategy but effective. It is shunned by the general public and media. However, history and logic are its defenders. Gold and silver are the best forms of money. Fiat money was only created in order to sidestep the government's debt problems, because they could print more money to pay off debts. This results in inflation. When a rate of return is stated, inflation is most likely not calculated into the return of the investment. This is a huge deception. *Inflation is a huge factor*! It does not matter how much percent gain you had if the underlying value of the dollar decreases just as much or more! The Federal Reserve has a monopoly on the monetary supply and sets artificial interest rates. It creates a long boom and bust cycle. However, gold is not always the best investment during certain periods, either. During time periods of this cyclical change, the best investment switches from stocks during an economic expansion, to gold during a consolidation period in the stock market. The time-period changes can be predicted by the use of the P/E ratio and the average sixteen-year period. I wrote this book because I think that this information is important for people to understand and it is a good alternative to the failed investment advice given by large investment companies and the media.

THE COMPLETE INVESTMENT PORTFOLIO

There are many variables that need to be considered. This is just a general guide to show you a historically-accurate investment strategy that is an alternative to what is usually out there, where ordinary investment advice has failed again and again. It will only be tested by time. The stock market, during consolidation periods, real estate, and other investments should be considered and may be advantageous. By no means does this book suggest that you put all your wealth into gold or stocks. It is simply a guide for you to understand economic fundamentals, effects of inflation, and monetary policy, so that you can make better decisions in your investments. It is an aid, not a guideline. Also, throughout the book, gold is referenced as the main precious metal. However, it is important also to consider other precious metals such as silver, platinum, and palladium. It is also important to consider various commodities besides just precious metals. Each has their respective qualities, which give them value. Diversifying into other precious metals and commodities at opportune times is a good way to reduce the risk of owning only one commodity or sector of the market. Remember, diversification not only between, but within, asset classes is important.

PROFESSIONAL HELP: THE COMPETENT INVESTMENT ADVISOR

You can find professional help with an investment advisor. However, it will be a task in itself to find a competent investment advisor. Most likely you will find better success with an independent investment advisor that is not working for a large firm. These advisers are not pressured by a large company and their fallacious strategies. Most large companies promote the "long-term investment" or "short-term gambling." Independent investment advisors work for themselves and therefore are not pressured to promote the usual failed investment strategies. Whether you are close to retirement, saving for education, or are an aggressive investor or conservative investor, all these needs will have an impact on your portfolio. It is wise to find professional help. It is also important to note the drastic changes in the price of gold. A competent investment advisor will know how to protect a client on the downside risk with put options and other such strategies. Here is an unfortunate example of a personal experience I had with an investment advisor from a large firm that emphasizes the need for an independent advisor.

When I was younger and just entering the financial services field, I sat at a desk of a senior financial advisor to learn from his "sales" experience. He pulled out a chart of a mutual fund that he was actively selling to his clients. It was impressive. While showing me the upward sloping chart folded out to cover his desk he said, "You see here, if you invested $10,000 in 1910, you would have six million dollars today!" Along with the visual chart, he made it sound great. But remember to factor in what we have previously learned. Who had $10,000 in 1910? That's like having $250,000 in today's dollars! So, no average person had that kind of money to invest for the long term upfront. Also, the time period he stated was over the span of ninety years! I'll be lucky to live that long, let alone earn money for ninety years! So you need to consider two things when evaluating information from conventional "historical gains" that are expressed by investment advisors and their companies:

1) Time period – How long is the time period? If it is a shorter time period, was it during an up-trend period or a consolidation period of the stock market?

2) Inflation – How has inflation affected the initial investment amount and what is the *real* return of the investment? *(Use the BLS Inflation Calculator)*

THE 25-PERCENT RULE

I recommend that approximately 25 percent of a total investment portfolio should *always* be in gold, other precious metals, or commodities like real estate, no matter what the time period suggests. If history is our guide, it tells us that fiat currencies will *always* fail. Sometimes, they fail very quickly. It can move so quickly that you won't be able to move your assets to another investment. In places like Germany, Zimbabwe, and other countries, the currency experienced extreme hyperinflation in a matter of months. Because of this, a private collection of physical precious metals, I believe, is a smart move to protect against that risk.

GERMAN REISHMARK U.S. DOLLAR EXCHANGE RATE

April 1919: 1 dollar: 12 marks
January 1923: 1 dollar: 17,000 marks
August 1923: 1 dollar: 4.621 million marks
October 1923: 1 dollar: 25.26 billion marks
December 1923: 1 dollar: 4.2 trillion marks

The other reason why I suggest that it may be advantageous to own 25 percent of physical gold or other commodities at all times is because of the long-term budgetary policies of the United States government and it's risk of default (whether that be default through contracts, inflation, etc). Here is our fiscal situation at the time of printing this book (it most likely has risen since):

- Over $110 *trillion* dollars in unfunded future government liabilities (social security, Medicare, Medicaid, etc)
- Over $13 *trillion* dollars of national debt
- Over $1 *trillion* dollars of state debts
- Over $1 *trillion* dollars of local government debts
- Over $15 *trillion* dollars in private citizen debts
- Interest to finance-expanding debt is rising!

Total Debt = Over $130 *trillion* in debt

TOTAL ASSETS (small business, corporations, household assets) = approximately $70 *trillion* dollars

If that doesn't ring an alarm bell in your gut, I don't know what will. It is obvious that we will have to inflate the currency in the future in order to cover our debts or outright default. If we sold *everything* in America, including real estate, stocks, and bonds, we would *still* be in debt $60 *trillion* dollars! Inflating the currency will increase the nominal value of small businesses, corporations, and household assets while, at the same time, the debt is paid off with the increased taxes that those rising valued assets bring. In order for the United States to survive financially, it is inevitable that there needs to be a strong inflationary period in order to make a big enough correction of our debts.

Chapter Eleven: Your Investment Portfolio

CONCLUSION

No one knows what the future holds. If any investment "guru" expresses their ability to foresee the future with certainty, ignore them. They may be right, but they may be wrong. But the blind confidence that they give you will hurt you more than help you. Every time a disaster or an economic crisis happens this becomes obvious. Supposedly the most "intelligent" person becomes hated because he is now wrong. Sometimes people *still* follow this person out of denial of the facts. No one can predict the future. We can do our best with the information provided. But even with the information, we are human and make mistakes and miscalculations that end up making our theories crumble. We are human.

Over the course of a century, wealth has been created in the United States at an accelerated rate. However, *inflation* is an important part of that monetary equation. What I hope this book has done is show you the difference between a *nominal* and *real* amount (or the difference between numbers and their purchasing powers). With this added information (which is often neglected in determining investment returns) a secret investment pattern has been revealed to you that uses that information. Only time will tell if it holds true.

SUGGESTED READING

The Wealth of Nations by Adam Smith

Writings: Jefferson edited by Merrill Peterson

Human Action: A Treatise on Economics by Ludwig Von Mises

Money Mischief by Milton Friedman

Inclined To Liberty by Louis E. Carabini

Broke by Glenn Beck

The Creature from Jekyll Island: A Second Look at the Federal Reserve by G. Edward Griffin

End the Fed by Ron Paul

The 5,000 Year Leap by W. Cleon Skousen

Principle & Interest: Thomas Jefferson and the Problem of Debt by Herbert Sloan

The Road to Serfdom by Frederick A. Hayek

The General Theory of Employment, Interest, and Money by John Maynard Keynes

Economics in One Lesson by Henry Hazlitt

Why Austrian Economics Matters by Llewellyn Rockwell Jr.

The Communist Manifesto by Karl Marx & Friedrich Engels

Atlas Shrugged by Ayn Rand

Suggested Websites & Associations

www.mises.org *Ludwig Von Mises Institute of Austrian Economics*

www.chrismartenson.com

www.usdebtclock.org

www.campaignforliberty.com

Visit www.danielkrug.com for more information

Suggested Reading